Rhoat

Merry Christmas

everyone

He is the King

PASSIONATE PEACE

PASSIONATE PEACE

The Art of Surrender

TERI FRANA

Fisher – Abide Education and Publishing
Des Moines

Passionate Peace © 2005 by Teri Frana

ISBN # 0-9771542-0-3

Printed in association with Fisher-Abide Education and Publishing, Des Moines, Iowa. Please direct inquiries to info@Fisher-Abide.com.

Printed in the United States of America

To Mom and Dad –

Through you I've been born and born again after you led me to the One. You relentlessly showed me that love is truly the greatest of these. You've stuck by me with such tenacity that I know the meaning of perseverance. May you be blessed with abundant peace.

TABLE OF CONTENTS

INTRODUCTION

Give me the love that leads the way, the faith that nothing can dismay,
The hope no disappointments tire, the passion that will burn like fire,
Let me not sink to be a clod: Make me Thy fuel, Flame of God.
Amy Carmichael

I couldn't move. My arms and legs wouldn't budge. I felt like I was trapped in a block of cement. My heart was as immobile as my body as it sat like a stone in my chest. I was afraid I'd never feel anything again.

The events of the last couple of years kept going through my head as I sat there on the couch. It wasn't a pretty sight. Those years had been the toughest I had ever endured. It seemed like every time I thought things couldn't get worse, they did. Instead, I started saying to myself, "Things will get worse, just wait." My cynicism was becoming a habit.

I had grown ice cold. I was cried out, talked out and prayed out. I felt distant from my friends and family and especially from God. My walk with Christ had come to a dead stop. I was completely paralyzed in my heart. I felt no emotion; no joy, no peace, no sadness, no anger. I had nothing left but emptiness.

So there I sat on the couch unable to move. I prayed, "Lord, please release me. I'm dead inside anyway." I closed my eyes and waited and waited some more. When my end didn't come, I decided that God had stopped listening. At that point, I didn't even try to talk myself out of it. I just sat there.

The worst part of feeling this way, for me, was that I had no passion for anything. There was no fire burning in my heart. No bounce in my step. No reason to get out of bed. No purpose for my existence. It was very lonely, lost feeling.

I found out that God had a reason for me to be at the place where I felt dead. I know, I know. I should have known that God has a purpose for everything. But, sitting on that couch, I just couldn't get that through my head. But, yes, that day I found out the reason for the suffering. God wanted me to experience a stone cold heart in order for me to understand

1

the power of a passion-filled heart. That day, down to my last drop of energy, God refilled my tank and gave me a complete "God overhaul."

How it happened, I'm not sure. It's sometimes difficult to understand God's ways. All I can tell you is that I once felt dead, and through the Holy Spirit, I was revived. I remember thinking to myself, "I wish I could run away from it all, but I'll never be able to run away from God. I give up." I finally surrendered. That was the moment I felt His presence draw near.

God rushed in to give me just what I needed to get up off the couch and take my first few steps toward healing. Over the next few weeks and months, He led me down the path that has now become this book. Bit by bit, He has taught me that having a passionate purpose is what gives meaning to life. Passionately seeking Him in all things and surrendering everything else is the only goal worthy of my time.

Christ asked a few ordinary men to drop their fishing nets, surrender the only life they knew, and single-mindedly follow Him. They responded to Him and incredible things happened. Through their walk with Christ, they became extraordinary.

When we surrender, we allow Christ to transform us in incredible ways. He works within us and overflows to those around us. Look the simple fisherman Simon, named Peter, the day Christ first asked him to drop his nets and follow. Observe Peter through his journey with Jesus up to his betrayal of his teacher (Any of the Gospels). Then watch Peter's powerful ministry after Christ's death (Acts). Peter was an ordinary man until he was forever changed by Christ, and molded into a passion-filled apostle. God is constantly taking "regular Joes" who surrender themselves to Him and transforming them into something spectacular.

God is passionate about His transformations. He will patiently pursue us to the ends of the earth if need be. He wants us to follow Him and he'll wait until we figure that out. He'll give us just what we need along the way to help us, and He won't give up. He loves us that much.

Love is patient and kind. Love is not jealous or boastful or proud or rude. Love does not demand its own way. Love is not irritable, and it keeps no record of when it has been wronged. It is never glad about injustice but rejoices whenever the truth wins out. Love never gives up, never loses faith, is always hopeful, and endures through every circumstance.
1 Corinthians 13:4-7NIV

This is how God loves us, each day, every moment, in good times and bad. He loves us with reckless abandon. Nothing can change the way He feels about us. That's passion.

2

We can become people share God's passion. We can drop our fishing nets and leave everything behind to follow Christ. We can drop whatever we are clinging to and allow Him to transform us. The journey may not be filled with happiness and comfortable circumstances. It will, however, be filled with peace, joy and God's abundant love.

The key to all of this is your surrender. Once you unlock the door, Christ will lead you to places you've never even dreamed of going. The peace that will fill you is beyond comprehension and your life will never be the same. Are you ready to find passionate peace?

Because Thy lovingkindness is better than life, my lips shall praise thee.
Psalm 63: 3 NKJ

CHAPTER ONE

YOUR
WILL
BE DONE

God has landed on this enemy-occupied world in human form...The
perfect surrender and humiliation was undergone by Christ: perfect
because He was God, surrender and humiliation because He was man.
C.S. Lewis

I'm writing this with my laptop precariously perched on what's left of my lap. You see, each month that passes, my belly keeps growing into my lap, as today I'm starting my ninth month of pregnancy. Very soon, the little being inside of me will burst forth and begin her new life on the earth.

I've been sitting here on the front porch, enjoying the first warm day we've had as March comes in like a lamb. I'm thinking about the little lady that I will soon get to meet. My mind has been filled with peaceful, blissful thoughts about how she'll smell and how soft her skin will be. AAAHH! Like a Gerber commercial.

In the midst of this lovely dream, another thought pushes its way in to disturb my bliss. This baby has to come out of me somehow. The logistics of this feat tends to defy comprehension. This moment was inevitable. No pregnant woman can escape it. It's the moment when you realize there is no turning back. One way or another, a seven to nine pound bundle of joy with arms, legs, elbows and a skull must exit my body.

Dread has started to creep in. True, I've had two other children. But that does little more than make me realize how absolutely insane I was to want another one! Will someone please explain to me what I could have possibly been thinking?

I know the drill. "What a blessing. When it's all done, it will be so worth it, you just forget about the pain." I must admit, I've said this myself to expectant mothers. However, I must reiterate that none of this is bringing much peace right now. This baby is coming out one way or another! I simply don't like any of the options that I have been given. I wonder if I could get a second opinion?

Why have I spent your precious time detailing the thoughts in my head? Because I think it is relevant to this chapter. Please humor me another couple of minutes – there is a point – I promise. Fast forward a very short time from now, and I will be filled with joy. I will have given birth to a new life, born of my flesh. Her birth will bring a renewing of all of us as we grow to love her more each day.

However, I don't have a "real-time remote" so I can't stop and start my life with the click of a button. Sometimes I wish I had a "scene selection" option like on a DVD, so I could select whatever scene from my life I wanted to play and skip over any scenes that I can do without. But, I don't. I can't fast forward just yet. I must go through this next month.

I know there will be more pain and suffering. I'm anticipating the scary moments and times when I don't think I'll be able to make it. Here I am asking God to not make me drink of this cup. "Lord, could you find me a better path? What about just blinking me out of my body for a while? Maybe I could drift weightless above my earthly body while it lays there in labor?" It could happen!

My last few moments of doubts have made me wonder what was going through Jesus' mind when He was in the Garden of Gethsemane the night before His death. He was about to offer rebirth to all mankind. Complete victory was only a few days away. He would change the world forever. In fact, it was the very reason He was born. He knew what He would have to do this since the beginning of time. Yet, He was going to have to endure horrific pain and suffering before that could happen.

I often wonder exactly what took place in the garden that night. Jesus had to find a way to embrace His destiny with all his heart, mind, soul and strength. At that moment, it was the last thing He wanted to do, but it was the very thing being asked of Him.

Jesus might have thought He was ready. Just days before, Jesus had calmly warned people about what would happen; although none of them truly understood. He had accepted the woman's anointing of perfume from her alabaster jar in preparation for His burial. Earlier that very evening, He and His disciples had an intimate dinner designed to say goodbye and impart final words of wisdom. He should now be ready to leave this earth. I have a feeling as the moment drew closer; the realization of what was to come was closing in on Him. There was no turning back.

That night, the burden was too much for Him to bear alone. Jesus wanted to be surrounded by a beautiful garden and loving friendship to help strengthen Him. Jesus desperately needed to talk to God; He needed reassurance before He would be able to face His destiny. So, Jesus went to be alone with His Father in the solace of the Garden of Gethsemane.

IN THE GARDEN

The night is still and clear. The warmth had left the air as the sun went down. Jesus feels the warmth leaving His heart as well. Greatly troubled; He calls his closest companions to sit with Him as He prays. He asks them for comfort and diligence. Tonight, He needs their strength.

He told them, "My soul is crushed with grief to the point of death. Stay here and watch with me."   *Matthew 26:38 NLT*

Jesus then walks to a quiet place and breathes in the beauty around Him. He knows He won't be on earth much longer. He thanks His Father for the loveliness surrounding him. In the very next moment, His mind grasps the bittersweet reality of the situation. He is not of this world. He is being called back to His Father. He is being asked to take His rightful place. He was only to be here a short time, but overwhelming sorrow grips Him as He prepares for His last day on earth.

Quickly He kneels. The ground is hard, but His knees are used to this act of surrender. His mind races with so many thoughts that He doesn't even notice the discomfort. His first thoughts are of what His Father is asking of Him. He must suffer at the hands of those who are not worthy of the dust beneath His feet. Endure untold atrocities. Be tortured at the hands of evil. He will do this with a peaceful, joy-filled heart and with a spirit of pure compassion and forgiveness. He will do this without bitterness, fear or doubt.

Jesus probably could have done these things with God's help. However, in addition to this unspeakable task, Jesus also knows that at the very moment when He would need the Father's strength the most, the Father will pull away. God will sacrifice His only beloved Son on the cross and leave Him alone to bear the weight of all the sins of this world; past, present and future.

As His mind races through these thoughts and images, His anguish is almost more than He can take. His whole body convulses at the thought of being without His Father's presence. He believes just to imagine the separation would be enough pain to end His life. Jesus finally speaks as the drops of blood drip down and hit the dirt.

"My Father! If it is possible, let this cup of suffering be taken away from me."   *Matthew 26:39a NLT*

He knows that God is the only one who could change the events that will take place. He weeps as He again is gripped with the reality of what needs to be done.

He pounds the ground in desperation and hunches over, resting His head on His arm as He weeps. The liquid in the cup is too bitter to drink. He clenches some dirt in His fist. He reels back onto his heels and looks up at the sky. He can barely whisper.

"Yet I want Your will, not mine."   *Matthew 26:39b NLT*

He feels no relief as He releases the dirt. He goes back to His friends to find comfort but finds them asleep, unable to keep their eyes open. His heart sinks. Jesus desperately needed His friends to understand the situation, to be watchful and alert. He looks at Peter. Jesus had longed for Peter's uplifting spirit to encourage Him. But, He found them asleep.

> *When he came back to his disciples, he found them sound asleep. He said to Peter, "Can't you stick it out with me a single hour? Stay alert; be in prayer so you don't wander into temptation without even knowing you're in danger. There is a part of you that is eager, ready for anything in God. But there's another part that's as lazy as an old dog sleeping by the fire."*   *Matthew 26:40-41 The Message*

Jesus looks away from them. Tonight He needs a trusted ally. Jesus knows the only One He could trust was waiting for Him in the garden. Without hesitation, Jesus goes alone to pray once more.

He can barely walk to His favorite place. His legs give way before He gets there and once again He is on His knees. Tears stream down His face as the anguish in His heart takes hold again. He can't find fresh words to speak, so He simply repeats the same prayer.

"O my Father, if this cup may not pass away from me, except I drink it..."   *Matthew 26:42a NKJV*

He falls forward with His face to the dirt. He pauses for a moment as His words echo in the air. Deep down in His spirit, Jesus realizes He will have to drink from this cup. His path is set and the Father's will is revealed. Jesus weeps again.

Jesus rocks back and forth on the ground. He once again clutches dirt with His fists. "My Lord, my Father, please minister to me and lend me your strength. I want your plan for me to be fulfilled more than I do not want this suffering." He pauses and tries to catch His breath as He says,

"...Thy will be done." Matthew 26:42b NKJV

Jesus rolls over on His back and looks up at the sky. He takes a long, deep breath. He opens His fists and allows the dirt to fall from them. Soon, He would rejoin His Father in heaven and find the fulfillment He so longs for. But, He will have to wait.

Again, He goes to His friends. Again, they have fallen asleep. He looks at them for a moment. His righteous anger flares briefly at their thoughtlessness. But, it is not yet their time to understand. Knowing their suffering would begin soon after His ends, He decides to let them rest. Quickly He goes back to pray to His Father.

"Father, You are the only One I can turn to. I praise You for Your faithfulness. I long to be with You once again." As He ponders what He will endure before this reuniting, His heart seizes up once more and grief fills Him. However, this time it subsides as quickly as it rose. He knows the right prayer, He knows what He needs to do, He knows what is at stake, and He has made His final decision to surrender. This time when He says, "...Your will be done", He says it with quiet determination. Just then, angels minister to Him and peace begins to overflow from within Him.

He stands up, looks at His hands and wipes the remaining dirt from them. He knows these very hands will be pierced. He takes His sleeve and wipes His brow. He knows it will be torn by many thorns. He pats His face dry, knowing soon He will be severely beaten. He straightens His tunic, which will be stripped from Him. His hand goes to His side which will be pierced to prove His death. He knows all of His suffering will fulfill prophecies given long ago.

He breaths deeply again and feels the anguish exiting His body with each exhale. As He breaths in, He feels God filling Him with strength and purpose. He fully understands that the victory over death will be won through His surrender and God's mighty power.

Just then, He hears voices in the garden. He looks around Him one last time to drink in the beauty. He then turns and goes out to meet His betrayers. When He receives the kiss that signals the beginning of His suffering and sacrifice, He is filled with the power of the Holy Spirit. He can look into the face of Judas with love and compassion because it is all part of the divine plan developed before creation. He knows the fulfillment of this plan will forever change the world. His commitment is complete and He is utterly at peace.

PERFECT SURRENDER

This beautiful, yet intense picture of surrender reveals how God, wrapped in man flesh, surrendered to the ultimate plan. He became nothing so that God could be everything. He shows us just how powerful surrender can be. It can change the world.

What about us? Is it realistic to think we can do this, too? It's not as far away from your reach as you may think. Success is not dependant upon our perfection, strength or ability. We are perfected through what Christ did on the cross as He died for the sins of the world and was resurrected three days later to win victory over death. His blood washed us clean as His resurrection offers us eternal life.

The only requirement is that we relentlessly give everything we are and everything we aren't to God. Then the Creator of the universe uses His power and might to work through us. He transforms our lives and we get to watch it happen.

We lay it all down in front of God, as Christ did in the garden. We give ourselves over completely. God fills us with confidence and assurance that He is sufficient. God fulfills His awesome plan as we follow His lead. We are left with perfect peace. This is His promise and it's only a passionate surrender away.

I have been put up on the cross to die with Christ. I no longer live. Christ lives in me. The life I now live in this body, I live by putting my trust in the Son of God. He was the One Who loved me and gave Himself for me.

Galatians 2:20 NLV

Questions to Ponder

1. What does it mean to surrender to God?

2. Why is the willingness to surrender to God important?

3. Why did God reveal this picture of surrender in the Garden of Gethsemane to us?

4. How can there be power in surrender?

CHAPTER TWO

OUR
ONLY
CHOICE

My dear Jesus, my Savior, is so deeply written in my heart,
that I feel confident, that if my heart were to be cut open and chopped to pieces,
the name of Jesus would be found written on every piece.
Ignatius

It's overwhelming! Today's world is filled with unlimited choices. Everyday we're faced with a barrage of options flying past us at light speed. Some days I can hardly catch my breath before the next day begins. I feel tired before I even get out of bed. The concepts of joy and peace seem as distant as the farthest galaxy.

The days slip by faster than we can count them. When we finally realize the roller coaster we're on, we become obsessed with finding ways to get off. We downsize and resize. We take pills to help calm our nerves, slow us down or speed us up. We read books about how to regain control. We might even think we "get it" for a short while, only to find that "it" slips through our fingers. Eventually we find ourselves spinning out of control again, losing sight of what's important as we get carried away in the whirlwind around us.

I THINK I CAN, I THINK I CAN

The most frustrating part of all of this is even though we are moving so fast and doing so much, it seems like it is never enough. No matter how hard I try sometimes, I still can't do all that I think I should. I neglect my husband. I don't do enough for my kids. I'm not involved enough at church. I don't send out my Christmas cards on time. I procrastinate on house cleaning. We never seem to be able to get ahead of the bills. It feels like there's never enough of me to go around.

Yet when I surveyed all that my hands had done and what I had toiled to achieve, everything was meaningless, a chasing after the wind; nothing was gained under the sun.   *Ecclesiastes 2:11 NIV*

So, we work harder and smarter. We reprioritize and adjust our schedules. I have spent most of my career helping people define personal goals and the steps to achieve them. Self-help had become my middle name. Some people had evened crowned me, "The queen of reorganization." I was great at getting rid of the "dead weight" in my schedule. I must have reorganized my life 100 different ways. I reinvented myself so many times I was starting to feel like Madonna!

A long time ago, I decided that I was going to be the "woman who had it all together." I was going to be the model Christian, be in perfect physical, mental and emotional shape, and be the best mom on the planet. So I aimed a little high, but I like to shoot for the stars.

For years, I think I tried every conceivable way of achieving of these goals. Sometimes, I would get up extra early (at around 4:30am) just so I could try to get it all done.

Physically, I worked-out like my life depended on it. I ate like a sparrow and watched the scale like an eagle. Mentally, I pushed myself to extremes, giving all that I had at work with every project. Emotionally, I committed myself to spending every spare moment I could with my family and friends. I worked so hard to build strong relationships that sometimes I went over the edge.

Spiritually, I pushed myself the hardest. I strived to know the Bible inside and out. I wasn't happy unless I was serving in almost every ministry and felt excruciating guilt if I didn't.

All of this while I was running the kids to all their activities, keeping a clean house, making sure we had groceries and keeping my finances in order as any good steward should.

I had it all together...for about three and a half minutes. The other 23 hours, 56 some odd seconds, I was out of control. I felt like a pin ball hitting all the bumpers. This would lead me back to the drawing board where I would reorganize my routine in effort to find that "perfect life balance." I thought if I could get into the right schedule, my life could be perfect.

I had only good intentions; the problem was when I had one area of my life in balance there were two other areas toppling down. I was always failing at something. I slept too long in the morning. Or I ate more than I should and didn't work-out enough. I wasn't praying or reading enough. I wasn't spending enough time with the kids or the house was falling apart around me.

I remember a lot of middle-of-the-night "melt-downs". There I was, lying there, curled into a fetal position crying myself to sleep, completely overwhelmed with guilt, shame and inadequacy.

Then I would hear God whispering to me, "You can do it – through me!" I heard the, "You can do it" part, and would feel renewed. I'd jump out of bed again with all my might and try it all again. Only to find myself melting down again a few days, weeks, months later in utter failure. I didn't understand that the power is in the, "through me" part. It's not about *my* performance; it's about His. I'm only the engine; Christ is the steam that makes it go. I was trying to make my engine get up that steep hill without any steam. No amount of, "I think I can, I think I can" is going to make that happen.

Back to the Basics

No matter what your goals and pursuits are, more than likely you have had an occasional "melt-down". You have probably felt overwhelmed, guilty or ashamed from time to time and wonder, "Will I ever get it? I want to follow His will. But, why is it so hard?"

You feel this way more often than you'd like. You might get drawn into the insanity of the world and find yourself in a fetal position trying to escape it. Or you might reach the breaking point and explode at the next person who gets in your way.

What I don't understand about myself is that I decide one way, but then I act another, doing things I absolutely despise.
Romans 6:15 The Message

Why does this happen? Maybe we're all just hopeless cases? Maybe we're weak of spirit and undisciplined? Maybe deep down, we just pretend to be good, but are just really fooling ourselves? Sometimes I think that lasting peace is only available to those "Joan of Arc" type Christians.

Let's be honest, sometimes it feels like God leaves us out here to fend for ourselves. He says He'll never leave us. He promises over and over again to answer our prayers. He says that we will never thirst again once we drink of Him. I've read it and heard it hundreds of times, but why is it hard to believe? I have to admit, I still feel parched sometimes.

If there is one thing I've learned about God, it's that when you're struggling the most, you need to go back to the basics. So often, we hear

Jesus telling us to become like children so that we can see the truth. If you feel stuck, frustrated or empty, it's time to look at yourself with the simple, straightforward innocence of a child.

First, we must strip away the surface "stuff" we have acquired throughout our lives and look at the utter core of our humanity. Take the focus off our happiness, grief, worries, securities, expectations, achievements and failures. Peel back the layers of possessions, circumstances, friendships, families, habits and careers. Scrape off our education, social status, clothes and make-up. Strip away all those things and stand in front of the mirror and what we see, without distraction, is our human core. Our humanness is all we came into this world with as a child, it's all we have today, and all we'll take with us when we leave this earth.

HUMAN CORE DEFINED

Life becomes much simpler once we strip away the "fluff" and focus on the naked human core. There have been numerous definitions flying around about specifically what makes up our human core. Let's dive in and determine a workable definition.

God created us with a mind, soul and spirit housed in a neat package called a body. Let's break this down and look closer:

- Our mind contains our thoughts and perceptions
- Our soul (called heart by some), contains our emotions and our human desires
- Our spirit (also called soul sometimes) is what longs to be reconciled with our Creator once again
- Our body is what houses all of these in a physical entity so we can move around in this world

Our Mind

Our mind is where our sequential and random thoughts are processed. Like a computer, our mind sorts through many aspects of life to find the practical, tangible beliefs to store in memory. How God created our brains to think is how we will perceive, process and retain the information that gets inputted. Some are practical people, common-sense thinkers who quickly solve problems thrown their way. Some have theoretical talents and can work their way through hypothetical thinking. Some brains were made to be able to handle abstract thought processes. Still, some are just black and white , "Ya gotta see it to believe it," thinkers. Each brain is created to function uniquely.

Our Soul

Our soul is sometimes called the heart, especially by non-Christians. This is where emotion comes from. Our human desires radiate from this place. It contains no logical, practical thought. The desires of our soul might tempt us to stop at Dairy Queen for that luscious chocolate on chocolate dipped cone ten times a week. We're in trouble when we allow our souls to control most of our actions. There are usually plenty of consequences we experience.

Our soul also contains some of what makes up our personality. What God put in us; longings, desires, passions. For example, I really enjoy being around other people. I like talking to everyone I meet. My husband is more of an introvert. He likes being alone and he doesn't have to talk to every person he stands beside in line.

One of my greatest desires is to be in the mountains. I come alive when I'm on a snow-capped mountain gazing down into the valley. My husband thinks mountains are ok, but loves the ocean. Put him on a beach and that is heaven to him. Why do we love some things and not others? I can't explain it. It's just how God made us.

Our Spirit

Until we accept Christ, our spirit works with God to call us back to Him. It's the part in each of us that knows there is something more to this life. It's the empty place that can only be filled by God. Everyone who breathes knows there is something....something else. Something we cannot see.

The heavens are telling of the greatness of God and the great open spaces above show the work of His hands. Psalm 19:1 NLV

The spirit stirs up a different kind of longing in us that's vast and deep. People seek to fill the spiritual void with just about anything that gives them that momentary comfort. It seems that comfort and happiness are the most important personal goals today. It never works! No matter what we try we can never seem to fill what the spirit craves. God places that within us so we will ultimately seek Him. Reconciling with our Creator is the only way to complete the spirit.

Once we accept Christ, our spirit is where the Holy Spirit takes up residence. It serves as our guide and counselor. This is the part of our human core that gets renewed within us upon salvation. Our spirit transforms and becomes "reborn"!

Flesh gives birth to flesh, but the Spirit gives birth to spirit. You should not be surprised at my saying, "You must be born again."
John 3:6-7 NIV

Once this transformation happens, you start seeing beautiful things creep into your life. You start experiencing love, joy and peace in ways you've never felt before. If you aren't experiencing these in your life right now, it's because you haven't truly surrendered your humanness. Once you lay down all of yourself before God, He then begins to water and nurture what is within your spirit. When this happens, watch out! You begin acting out from what God is doing within you. Surrendering your humanness is the key which unlocks the wonder.

Our Body

The body is what holds it all together. It's made up of those scientific, physiological mechanisms which are easy to pick apart to see how they work. The body is much like a car. It needs fuel (food) to run. The better the fuel, the better it runs. It needs care and maintenance to check for potential problems. There are all different makes, models, styles and colors. They're perfect and smell good when they are new. They start to fall apart and rust as they age. Once this happens, no amount of cosmetic work can ever make the car completely new again.

Just as with the body, the performance of the car greatly depends on the way the driver handles it. Similar cars can react very differently to the same situations based on the instructions from the driver. If a driver pushes the car too hard for too long, it breaks down sooner than a driver who takes more care. Reckless drivers can cause many consequences to himself and others. Considerate drivers make traffic run smoothly.

The Heart of the Matter

All of these components; mind, soul, spirit and body work together to determine our free-will choices. We need to engage all of the components to make the best choices and we typically suffer consequences when we neglect to use all the parts. For the purposes of this book, we will call these components of the human core the "heart" of a human. Life's choices become much less complicated when we strip away other distractions and simply focus on the core of our humanness, our heart.

PROGRAMMED PERCEPTIONS

At the base level of existence, what goes on within our hearts is automatic. You can think of it as running on "auto-pilot", made up of our brain connected via the central nervous system to the rest of our body. This system works together to do the sub-conscious activities it takes to exist; breathing, pumping blood, digesting and reacting with basic survival instincts to what our senses are picking up. These functions go on without much conscious thought.

A large part of what happens within our heart is perpetuated by our past experiences, our perceptions, our self-image and foundational beliefs. What our parents taught us to be like, what life has taught us to be like, and the beliefs we hold true can greatly impact our free-will choices. Whatever gets "programmed" into us throughout our lives greatly determines how we think, act and react. We can call these our "programmed perceptions."

Help! It's Stuck and I Can't Get It Off!

Our programmed perceptions just kind of "stick" to us. For example, if you were bullied by a tall, blonde-haired athletic kid in school, chances are, as an adult, you are uncomfortable around tall, blonde-haired athletic types whether you know them or not. Another example is if a teacher embarrassed you in front of the class for being tardy and called you slow. Fifty years later, you might still believe that you always respond in a slow manner, even if that isn't how others perceive you.

Here is an example you might relate to: my mom always wanted me to finish eating all the food on my plate before I left the table. As an adult, I felt guilty if I wasted any food, whether it was good for my health or not. These types of experiences seem to just stick with us and become part of the way we live our life.

Over time, we rarely stop to wonder why we are responding in a certain way. These responses become such a habit that we continue to react as we always have. It's as if we are "programmed" like a computer; deep down in our circuits in binary code. I had to tell myself over and over again that it was okay to stop eating when I was full and I had no reason to feel guilty for throwing away the rest of my food from my plate. My binary code had to be rewritten to accept the new inputs. Believe it or not, it took awhile to convince myself.

An obvious example of a programmed perception is that of a person suffering from anorexia. No matter how thin they become, they still see themselves as overweight. They have a deeply embedded code programmed into them to believe they are fat. It's nearly impossible to change their perception; not the scale, not the mirror, nor their family and friends telling them they are thin; not even the doctors telling them they are harming their bodies seem to help change the way they view themselves. It takes extremely hard work and a lot of reprogramming to get them to change their view of their bodies.

CONSCIOUS DECISION

Conscious, free-will decisions are also generated from within our heart. To come to a conclusion or decision, we use all the components of our heart. First, we examine our souls (our emotions and desires). Then, we use our minds (our thoughts and perceptions) to think through the different options available to us in our current circumstances. Our bodies can play a part in our decision depending on the needs of the situation (if we're hungry or cold, for example.) Our spirit can have an enormous impact in our decision making if we in-tune with the Spirit's leading as we seek God's direction in our lives.

We typically will go back-and-forth between all of these components until we feel comfortable with moving forward. While all of this is going on within our human core, we view this interaction through the lenses of our programmed perceptions until we develop a conclusion.

Let's look at an example of the process that goes on within our heart to make a conscious decision. Here's an example of a process that happened to me just the other day.

It was Saturday and both of my teenage kids had plans at different times with different friends. My husband had plans for what he wanted to accomplish in the garage, and I had developed a personal plan of attack for my day. The dilemma was to determine how we were going to work it all out and still feel like we got somewhere. Here is what used to happen within my heart:

(mind says) There is no way it's all going to get done.
(soul says) That's it! I'm overwhelmed! Let's do something fun instead!
(spirit says) Why don't you pray about it?
(mind says) BUT, we'll have no clean clothes unless I do laundry. The house is a pit and what are we going to have for dinner if I don't get to the store?
(programmed perceptions say) What a slouch you are! You should have worked harder during the week, then you wouldn't have left everything for today.

(soul says) I feel guilty.

(mind says) The kids just have to realize that you aren't their chauffeur all the time. They will have to help with the chores and just wait for another time to be with their friends. It's only logical.

(programmed perceptions say) They are going to be mad! You never do enough for them. You're not being a very good mom.

(spirit says) Why don't you ask God for help?

(mind says) Maybe we should work out a compromise? The kids can help with some of the chores, your husband can take them one way and you can pick them up.

(programmed perceptions say) Your husband had plans for his day. You should be able to get the rest done yourself. See, you always have to ask for help. You're being lazy!

(soul says) I give up! I'll never get it all together.

(spirit says) God will help you work out the compromise. Trust Him and your family to help.

(programmed perceptions say) God doesn't have time for such small problems.

These thoughts and feelings whirled around in my head for maybe only a split second. Being overwhelmed and having to make choices between the wants and needs of my family and other life obligations was one of my "hot buttons." It was a place that would cause me great stress. This example shows how our core components work together to derive a conclusion and the important role our programmed perceptions play in the interaction.

God Makes It Simple

The process of conscious decision doesn't need to be so complicated. God didn't intend it to be that way. Remember He asks us to be like children. He intended the activity within our heart to take much less of an effort. He offers us only one choice between two options. I used to use this technique with my kids when they were young. "Ok. We need to pick up this room before we go outside. So, do you want to pick up the toys first or the books?"

This is war, and there is no neutral ground. If you're not on my side, you're the enemy; if you're not helping, you're making things worse.
Matthew 12:30 The Message

God wants to make it that simple for us. When we strip away all the surface distractions of this world, we can see He makes our options to use our free-will quite straightforward. He offers us the choice between only two options; *do we choose to follow Jesus or do we choose to crucify Him*? God is very clear with us. You cannot follow God and follow something else at the same time. It's either one or the other. If we do not follow Christ, by default, we have chosen to crucify Him.

This is a harsh reality that many people are uncomfortable with, but reality it is, none the less. No matter what we do, humans cannot escape from the fact that God created us. We can ignore it, but it does not change the situation. There is no in-between, no gray area. It is, therefore, one of the seemingly few things in our lives that is black or white; if you are not for God, you are against Him.

Why does God make it so black and white? Why does He give us free-will when there are only two options? The short answer is – *He loves us beyond our understanding.* He knows that our rightful place is to live with Him in heaven for all of eternity. However, He didn't create us to be puppets which simply move when He pulls the strings. Rather, He created us in His image to be His beloved children.

For whom He foreknew, He also predestined to be conformed to the image of His Son, that He might be the firstborn among many brethren.
Romans 8:29 NKJ

I used to struggle quite often with the lies like, "You're a bad mom" and "You never do enough." It was deeply embedded binary code within my heart which was very hard to reprogram until I started stripping away my surface distractions. It's not about how much I can do; it is only about what God wants to do through me. From God's standpoint that is the only question which needs answered; do you follow me or not? Let's examine the same thought process after reprogramming the negative binary code and exposing the situation to God's simple truth:

(mind says) How are we going to get done all of this done?
(programmed perceptions say) It doesn't all have to get done. God will help you. He has already made a plan for the day. Just ask Him.
(mind says) Lord, I have chosen to follow You and this day is Yours. What would you have me do?

(spirit says) You need to work out a compromise. Talk to your husband. Ask the family to come together and talk about what needs to be done and how best to accomplish it. The kids will learn more about teamwork. Your husband enjoys helping you and you'll be able to accomplish everything that's needed today.
(programmed perceptions say) God always comes through. His promises are true.
(soul says) I feel peaceful. I know it'll all work out.
(mind says) Thank you, Lord!

Can you see how there is much less garbage going on? Deep within our hearts, we can quickly choose to follow Him in each situation; less struggle, less hassle, less negative thoughts, less confusion! Do you also see that the nagging, negative pre-programmed responses have now been changed to empowering, peaceful thoughts about God?

God makes it simple to use our free-will wisely. Our Father knows the only way to true and lasting peace is through a relationship with Him. He even gave us a fleshly example of ultimate sacrifice in order to show us how much He loves us. He only asks that we follow Jesus who was created to go before the Father on our behalf. Therefore, God designed it so we only have to choose between two options; follow Christ or not.

Can You Make This Hotter?

Once we have decided to follow Christ, God makes it even easier. God uses the life of Christ to show us how we too can live utterly surrendered. He boils it down and asks us to answer only one question: *to what degree are we willing to follow Him?* Do we follow Christ with all of our human core?

> *Jesus answered, "The foremost is, 'HEAR, O ISRAEL! THE LORD OUR GOD IS ONE LORD; AND YOU SHALL LOVE THE LORD YOUR GOD WITH ALL YOUR HEART, AND WITH ALL YOUR SOUL, AND WITH ALL YOUR MIND, AND WITH ALL YOUR STRENGTH.'"* Mark 12:29-30 NASB

Or will we follow Him only when it is convenient to do so? God calls us to follow Christ with everything we are. He wants us to pursue Him passionately (hot). He would rather have us choose to be cold (not following Him) than be somewhere in the middle.

I know your deeds, that you are neither cold nor hot. I wish you were either one or the other! So, because you are lukewarm—neither hot nor cold—I am about to spit you out of my mouth.

Revelation 3:15-16 NIV

Are you stoking up those raging fires of your heart? Is your heart cold as ice toward God? Or do you keep things tepid and safe? How you respond to the question may greatly impact your ability to surrender.

DROP YOUR NETS AND FOLLOW

The more we pursue a relationship with Christ, the more of ourselves He asks us to give up. This is the key to following Him with all our heart. His most devoted followers, His apostles, were asked to sacrifice everything. They were asked to "drop their nets" and leave the only life they had ever known. They couldn't take anything but the clothes on their backs. They didn't know where they were going or how long it would take to get there. They had no idea what would happen or where their next meal would come from. They were being asked to let go and surrender to the One who was leading. When these simple fishermen dropped their nets, they chose to be "red-hot" followers.

As Jesus was walking beside the Sea of Galilee, he saw two brothers, Simon called Peter and his brother Andrew. They were casting a net into the lake, for they were fishermen. "Come, follow me," Jesus said, "and I will make you fishers of men." At once they left their nets and followed him.

Matthew 4:17-23 NIV

Can you guess the reason God asks us to give so much of ourselves? *IT IS MUCH LESS DISTRACTING!* The more you surrender, the more clarity you have. The less you have to concern yourself with on this earth, the more concerned you become with God. The more you simplify and let go, the more peace you will enjoy. We're not only talking about material possessions. "Drop your nets" also means to willingly surrender all of our goals, desires, fears and frailties.

Till That's All

All I wanna do is give my life to You
And let Your will be done, till that's all I wanna do.
Ginny Owens

Our whirlwind life becomes much less overwhelming when we recognize that our only goal should be God's will. The beautiful thing in surrendering is that's all God asks us to do. He didn't say, "Drop your nets and follow me. *AND* you must think perfect thoughts. *AND* you must provide for every needy person you run into. *AND* show up for every service at church. *AND* say all the right things in every situation without fail. *AND* memorize every verse in the Bible and be able to recite it upon every applicable situation." No, He simply said, "Follow me."

Passionate followers realize that all you have to do is to choose to follow Him, then *He* will direct your paths in your righteous walk. He will provide you the strength and wisdom you need. Once you decide to follow Him, He is the steam that runs your engine and you are left with perfect, powerful peace.

> *For God is working in you, giving you the desire to obey Him and the power to do what pleases Him.*   *Philippians 2:13 NLT*

God makes it simple. When we strip away our surface distractions, look into our human core and look closely at our God-given free-will, we will see that our only choice is the degree to which we surrender ourselves. It is not our choice to be human. We can't choose to be God. After all, we are human and certainly not God. *Therefore, our only choice is to surrender our humanness to the One who is God.* We must learn to say, "Your will be done" in every circumstance. When we single-mindedly follow Christ, we can expect an adventure.

> *This resurrection life you received from God is not a timid, grave-tending life. It's adventurously expectant, greeting God with a childlike "What's next, Papa?"*   *Romans 8:15 The Message*

Questions to ponder:

1. Why does God ask us to passionately "drop our nets"?

2. Why does God say if we aren't for Him we are against Him?

3. What distracts you from God?

4. What does surrender mean to you?

CHAPTER THREE

EASY AS 1, 2, 3, REPEAT!

Just as a servant knows that he must first obey his master in all things, so the surrender to an implicit and unquestionable obedience must become the essential characteristic of our lives.
Andrew Murray

Does the word "surrender" conjure up images of wounded soldiers waving white flags and pleading for mercy? Do you see criminals who give themselves up to police after tiring of running? Does it make you think of weak people offering no resistance against an oppressive force? That is not the way God views surrender. To Him, surrender does not mean giving up, but *giving in* to His ultimate love. It means letting go of the control of our lives and allowing His mighty power to work in our lives.

OH! That's all! Well, it sounds easy enough. Why *wouldn't* we allow God full control over our lives? So, how do we do it? What does it take to "drop our nets" and obsessively follow Him? How do we say, "Your will be done" in every circumstance and mean it? Here's the secret: realize that it's Christ's job is to lead; our job is to follow. Live by this truth and then we will have complete peace. Easy right? *Riiiiight....* If only it were that easy to do!

No, it's not as easy as it sounds. One of the most incredible things about being loved by God is that He always provides a way to help us. He knows that it's not easy. God understands our frailties. He knows us better than we know ourselves.

Just as a father has compassion on his children, so the LORD has compassion on those who fear Him. For He Himself knows our frame; He is mindful that we are but dust. Psalm 103: 13-14 NASB

If I Had a Hammer

If I had a hammer
I'd hammer in the morning
I'd hammer in the evening
All over this land.   *Lee Hays and Pete Seeger*

The writer of this song sure thought they could accomplish a lot with the right tool! Our Father has given us the right tools for us to succeed. Our job is simply to use what He has given us. One of these tools is Bible stories. You won't find a much better "hammer" than the picture of Christ in the Garden of Gethsemane. Let's look at it again and glean some practical steps.

Then Jesus brought them to an olive grove called Gethsemane, and He said, "Sit while I go ahead to pray." He took Peter and Zebedee's two sons, James and John, and He began to be filled with anguish and deep distress. He told them, "My soul is crushed with grief to the point of death. Stay here and watch with me."

He went on a little farther and fell face down on the ground, praying, "My Father! If it is possible, let this cup of suffering be taken away from me. Yet I want Your will not mine." Then He returned to the disciples and found them asleep. He said to Peter, "Couldn't you stay awake and watch with me even for one hour? Keep alert and pray. Otherwise temptation will overpower you. For though the spirit is willing enough, the flesh is weak!"

Again He left them and prayed. "My Father! If this cup cannot be taken away until I drink it, Your will be done." He returned to them again and found them sleeping, for they just couldn't keep their eyes open.

So he went back and prayed a third time, saying the same things again. Then He came to His disciples and said, "Still sleeping? Still resting? Look, the time has come. I, the Son of Man, am betrayed into the hands of sinners. Up, let's be going. See my betrayer is here!"

Matthew 26:36-46 NLT

STEP ONE: GO TO YOUR FATHER IN PRAYER

Jesus was experiencing intense emotion. At no other time in the gospels do we see Him in such turmoil as we do in the garden. The key here is that as soon as Jesus realized His emotions were starting to overwhelm Him, He went directly to the Father in prayer. He did not hesitate or worry about dropping whatever He was doing. He did not mull over the situation with others, nor did He wallow in His fear all alone. He didn't make excuses and try to pretend He was fine. He went directly to speak to His Father.

He went on a little farther and fell face down on the ground, praying…
Matthew 26:39a NLT

So often we hear about the need for prayer. I often hear myself say, "I'll pray for you!" I mean it sincerely at the moment. Yet sometimes I realize days or weeks later that I forgot to do it. We know we need to. We know it's the best thing to do, yet, so often we forget to go before our Father immediately. However, prayer is crucial to turning up the heat of our spiritual walk.

STEP TWO: SURRENDER OUR HUMANNESS

Secondly, it is important to see that Jesus was completely honest about His feelings toward His situation. These verses show us that Jesus was full of sorrow over what was to come. He pleaded to be released from the suffering ahead, and He struggled to let go of His emotions. He wasn't ashamed of this. He was simply being human.

"My soul is grieved to the point of death…"   *Matthew 26:38 NLT*

We also see how He openly confessed His desires to God. He didn't want to go down that path unless He had to. He didn't doubt God's plan, He was simply asking for another option. "I know you said I would have to do this. But, just thought I'd double check first. Are you sure??" Again, this wasn't a sin. Sometimes we think we're distrusting God to double check to make sure we are still within His will. God doesn't resent us asking for the desires of our heart. He simply asks that we be willing to surrender even them to His will.

I know a man who left a very successful corporate career to pursue a home business. He was convinced at the time it was God's will for his life.

Almost two years later, the business hadn't taken off as he had anticipated and he experienced some doubt. So, he started to seek out different avenues. In his heart he said, "Lord, please continue to direct me. I will go where you lead. Just shut down any avenue you don't want me to go. I'm fine if You want me to continue with what I'm doing. I'm just double-checking. However, above all, I want your will not mine."

After much searching and questioning and surrendering, the path led him back to a corporate career. However, this time he has his career goals properly in line after his first priorities of God and family.

We are human! We will question and doubt. As long as our heart is still committed to following Him wherever He leads, we should not be afraid to ask. We just need to be willing to drop whatever we are clinging to and follow Christ.

STEP THREE: KNOW GOD

The third aspect to focus on is that Jesus never lost sight of God. He understood God's position over Him as the Father. Jesus had such a strong relationship with God He never doubted God's character. Jesus knew that His Father had a plan for His life that was bigger than anyone could see with their "worldly eyes". Jesus acknowledged God's ultimate power and love for Him.

> *"My Father! If it is possible, let this cup of suffering be taken away from me. Yet I want Your will not mine."*   *Matthew 26:39b NLT*

If we truly understood God's character, we would never wrestle with surrender. The creator of the universe is all-knowing, ever-present and eternal. He cannot lie, cheat, steal or be wrong. God is pure love and therefore is completely trustworthy. He cannot fail us! I know some of us have heard this a million times. But, do you really *believe* it? Do you really *know* it with every fiber of your being?

When we feel God's love to our very core, we cannot help but willingly give ourselves to Him. We must train our hearts to believe His truth. We need to reprogram the "binary code" of our human core to believe all of God's promises.

STEP FOUR: REPEAT UNTIL YOU HAVE PEACE

The last part of the picture is how Jesus continued to take His human frailties to God in prayer. He had to pray the same prayer repeatedly before the peace came. He had to do these steps *THREE* times before He was able to move forward and He was God in human flesh! He continually took it to the One who had total understanding. He took it to the only One who could provide the strength needed to stand and face His future.

So he went back and prayed a third time, saying the same things again.
Matthew 26:44 NLT

So, all this time you've spent surrendering over and over again hasn't gone to waste? NO! God expected us to repeat the steps over and over again. We won't "get it" all the time. We just won't. But, we can get better at it. The more we practice, the stronger we feel, and the less conflict we experience. We can relinquish the control in more and more areas of our life. There is no human alive today who lives totally surrendered in every circumstance. Strength comes from understanding and embracing that truth. We can never be perfect here on earth. We can only strive to keep allowing God to turn up the heat.

TRUE PEACE

True peace is only available to us when we drop our nets and follow Him. The longer we neglect to take the steps to surrender, the longer the confusion, fear, anger and emptiness will last. Even if we have to go through the steps every few minutes when things are really tough, peace has been promised to those who choose to passionately follow God.

Remember surrender, remember the rest.
Remember that weight lifting off of your chest
And realizing that it's not up to you
And it never was.   Sara Groves

Each time I finally let go of what I've been struggling with, I am filled in a way that is better than anything I have or will experience here on earth. That day on the couch when I was at the lowest point of my life, God rescued me. He pulled me out of my despair and gave me the strength to get up and take that first difficult step toward my future. I feel more powerful with each additional step. Since then, I've doubted a few times and had to repeat the steps to double check His will, but, the peace quickly returns as I stay focused on Him.

When you surrender, God lifts the heavy weight off your chest. Once you are relieved of this burden, you begin to be filled with confidence and strength. God gives you a great assurance that everything will be all right. You just *know* in your heart that God is in control. You realize that it's not up to you and it never was. There is great power in that.

Wake Up Sleepy Heads!

You see this power in the Garden of Gethsemane in Christ's determination as He stood up to meet His accusers. In the movie "The Passion of the Christ" I remember the scene in the Garden when Jesus looks down at His feet to see a serpent slithering around His feet. Jesus strikes the serpent dead with His heel. You can almost hear Jesus saying, "I will accept this task. I will follow You, my Father, no matter where You lead. I will fulfill Your plan for me. I know that You will provide for me."

> *Then He came to His disciples and said, "Still sleeping? Still resting? Look, the time has come. I, the Son of Man, am betrayed into the hands of sinners. Up, let's be going. See my betrayer is here!"*
>
> *Matthew 26:45 NLT*

From that moment on, Jesus never wavered, never doubted and never looked back. He was completely at peace and intensely focused on fulfilling God's purpose. It was clear in every action. You hear His passion in every word Jesus spoke.

> *"It is as you say."*   *Mark 15:2*

> *"I was born for that purpose. And I came to bring truth to the world. All who love the truth recognize that what I say is true."*   *John 18:37*

> *"Father, forgive these people, for they don't know what they are doing."*
>
> *Luke 23:34*

> *"It is finished!"*   *John 19:30*

Jesus became the strongest when He had completely surrendered. The least shall become the greatest. The servant will be the master. The meek shall inherit the earth. In Christ's surrender, He gained a Kingdom.

The greatest among you will be your servant. For whoever exalts himself will be humbled, and whoever humbles himself will be exalted.
Matthew 23:11-12 NIV

When we empty ourselves of the distractions of this world, we find our human core, our heart. When we choose to surrender all of our heart to God, *then* we find our true purpose. *He* will direct our paths into eternity. *He* will complete us in ways we never dreamed possible. The peace and fulfillment we long for is only a few steps away. It's simple. It's God. There is no way around it, surrender is certainly sweet.

Then Jesus said to His disciples, "If anyone desires to come after Me, let him deny himself, and take up his cross, and follow Me. For whoever desires to save his life will lose it, but whoever loses his life for My sake will find it. For what profit is it to a man if he gains the whole world, and loses his own soul? Or what will a man give in exchange for his soul?   *Matthew 16:24-26 NKJV*

Questions to ponder:

1.   Which do you think is the most important step of the process?

2.   What do you think would happen if you ignored one of the steps?

3.   Why do you think God tells us that the meek shall inherit the earth? Why is that important to God's plan?

CHAPTER FOUR

GO TO
THE FATHER

*Love is kindled in a flame, and ardency is its life. Flame is the air which
true Christian experience breathes. It feeds on fire; it can withstand
anything rather than a feeble flame; but when the surrounding
atmosphere is frigid or lukewarm, it dies, chilled and starved to its vitals.
True prayer MUST be aflame.*
E.M. Bounds

Prayer is the first step to surrender for a good reason. It's crucial. Our
relationship with God is ice-cold without it.

What do you think would happen if we took a camera and a microphone
to a busy street in Anytown, USA, and interviewed random people to ask if
they think prayer is important? My guess is that many of them would say,
"Of course."

I've heard many people say, "You're in our prayers", not necessarily just
from those who profess to be Christian. I've heard TV anchor men and
women say, "The nation prays for those hardest hit by this disaster." Even
Hollywood occasionally throws in a scene or two with someone talking to
God. Prayer seems to be one of those things that's deemed "acceptable" in
many social circles.

Those of us who have given their lives to Christ know that prayer is
critical in our Christian walk. Christ continually stressed the importance of
prayer. It has been the subject of countless sermons in churches. There are
literally hundreds of books on the subject. I would guess that prayer is one
of the most talked about subjects in Christian circles.

Why is it so important? Why is God so eager to converse with us?
Doesn't He already know everything we want to say? It's not as if we can
offer Him advice or comfort Him in any way. It's simply because God
desires a strong *relationship* with us. He cares about us that much. That's
the passion of His heart.

Look at any of your relationships. If you aren't having consistent, honest communication, your relationship is probably only lukewarm. Your bond won't grow richer unless you connect often with that other person. Without earnest, intimate conversation, there is no passion.

God wants us to share ourselves with Him and for us to get to know Him better. He wants our relationship to flourish. God already knows our hearts, but He asks us to open them to Him by our own free-will. The more we connect with Him, the more we get to know and trust Him. He wants to guide our lives to wondrous things. He has an incredible plan for us, if we just allow Him into our lives. It shows how completely He loves us.

Before they call I will answer; while they are still speaking I will hear.
Isaiah 65:24 NIV

A Life of Prayer

Because it was an integral part of His life, Jesus showed us how important prayer was to Him. He went alone to pray. He prayed out loud. He taught us how to pray. The last words He said were cried out in prayer.

The Jesus shouted, "Father, I entrust my spirit into Your hands." And
with those words He breathed His last.   *Luke 23:46 NLT*

It is a consistent theme in the books written of His life. We already saw His desperate prayers in the Garden of Gethsemane. Here are a few more examples of answered prayer:

- Jesus wandered in the desert for 40 days with God. (Matthew 4:1-11)
- He prays alone in Galilee. (Mark 1:35)
- Jesus prays before choosing the twelve disciples. (Luke 6:12)
- He prayed in the hills after feeding 5,000. (John 6:15)
- He taught us how to pray with the Lord's Prayer. (Matthew 6:5-13)

Obviously, God wants us to communicate. He wants us to talk to Him and He wants us to listen for His leading. He wants our prayer to be aflame! Yet, He patiently waits for us to pick up the phone and dial.

You may be thinking, "I hear you. I think this sounds true. I just haven't experienced it." It may seem to you that He is not listening. You may think that answered prayer is what happens to other people. You may wonder what you are doing wrong or you may question the power of prayer. Read on. You will find some answers, encouragement and practical steps on how to overcome the barriers. Prayer is crucial to a surrendered life. There is no peace without it.

BARRIERS

It should be the easiest thing we ever do, talking with our Creator, but, for many people, prayer is difficult. Many people battle with finding the time to be alone and undistracted. Others find prayer intimidating because they aren't sure how to do it. Still others doubt whether prayer really makes a difference. Regardless of what you struggle with, God provides a way to make it easier.

The "I Don't Have Time" Cha-Cha

Many Christians have a hard time finding time for quality prayer. I know this is the biggest barrier for me. Life seems so busy at times it's hard to remember to take that quiet time with Him. And I do mean hard! We have so much going on with day-to-day activities and frustrations that we neglect our conversation with God. When I feel completely overwhelmed, that is a sign for me I've been too busy to talk to my Father. That is my cue to slow down and spend more time with Him.

If you find it difficult to make the time to be alone in prayer with God, the best defense is commitment. Start small at first and work up. Commit yourself to spending five minutes with God before getting out of bed and before going to sleep. Don't allow any distractions. Discipline yourself to think of nothing but God during that time. Train yourself to focus daily on your Creator. Just as with any new exercise, it takes commitment, discipline and consistency. You might be able to "jog" one block the first day, but over time, you will work up to three miles a day. Stay committed and keep going even when it gets rough. It's about holding nothing back; even our busyness can be surrendered to Him and He will help.

Are you tired? Worn out? Burned out on religion? Come to me. Get away with me and you'll recover your life. I'll show you how to take a real rest. Walk with me and work with me - watch how I do it. Learn the unforced rhythms of grace. I won't lay anything heavy or ill-fitting on you. Keep company with me and you'll learn to live freely and lightly.
Matthew 11:28-30 The Message

The "Just Keep Talking" Shuffle

Another barrier to prayer is getting hung-up on the words we use. We feel embarrassed if our prayers aren't full of "Christian-ese" wise and proper idioms. We listen to others who say things just right, and feel inadequate. We find ourselves more concerned with sounding good than with speaking from the rawness of our heart. I know this is a barrier many people face; they just don't know what to say and it makes them feel very uncomfortable and awkward.

The good news is that God doesn't care that we use complete, clear sentences. He isn't concerned with our grammar. He isn't concerned that we fill in all the details, or get to the point. God just wants us to be...us.

When you pray, don't babble on and on as people of other religions do. They think their prayers are answered only by repeating their words again and again. Don't be like them, because your Father knows exactly what you need even before you ask Him!   Matthew 6:7-8 NLT

There is an old recipe that I was told to use when praying. Remember to praise God first and foremost, count your blessings, make your request to God for others, and then for yourself (making sure you take care of any thing that needs to be confessed and ask for forgiveness.)

I find it difficult to have a lengthy prayer. I get talking too much and lose track of where I am. I take more tangents than a geometry class! So, I have to mix up the order and break it into manageable pieces throughout my day.

I try to remember to praise Him first thing in the morning. "Lord, you are AWESOME!" I try to count my blessings at night before I go to bed. "I thank you for all that you are doing in my life. Especially that one thing today – that was too cool!!" I try to remember others in prayers when I'm on e-mail or as the need comes up. Lastly, I think about my situation and needs when I'm in the shower. "Today will be a hard day Lord. I'm gonna need your help BIG time on this. Please fill me with You while You empty me of me."

As you can tell, my conversations with Him are pretty laid back. I don't get hung up much on the words. I know He looks into my heart for the meaning behind the words. God will understand even your ranting. Practice is the best cure for your insecurity. The more you pray, the easier it will become a habit for you.

The "Is This Thing On?" Tango

Have you ever felt dry in your prayer life? Have you ever wondered if the "microphone" we were using to talk to God was actually on? Or if the cell phone tower was in service? "Hello? Hello? Can You hear me?" It is as if the open lines of communication suddenly were turned off. This is a common barrier with many Christians.

Sometimes we are the ones who have tuned God out and sometimes God is just giving us a little room to grow. Persistence is the best defense against the silence. Keep trying and don't give up. Search your heart and ask God to reveal anything that is holding you back from a full prayer life. Trust that He hears you even though you may not believe it.

During some of my most difficult times in life, God seemed to be the most silent. Sometimes it was me not listening. Sometimes, it was God simply allowing a little breathing room for me to test my wings. It seems like at that point, I begin to fall down in my prayer life. I begin to think, "Well, it ain't working!" That is my signal to know that it's only my human frailties seeping out and it's time to reconnect with my Father.

Even when we struggle with prayer, God, once again, comes through to help us. He's given the gift of the Holy Spirit to intercede for us. God makes it nearly impossible for us to fail. We don't even have to know what or how to pray. He's got us covered!

In the same way the Spirit also helps our weakness; for we do not know how to pray as we should, but the Spirit Himself intercedes for us with groanings too deep for words; and He who searches the hearts knows what the mind of the Spirit is, because He intercedes for the saints according to the will of God.   Romans 8:26-27 NASB

HEARING THE WHISPER

What's important to God is the relationship. One part of that relationship is our conversing with Him. The other important part is *listening* for His reply back to us. Sometimes we get so carried away with talking, we forget to listen. Sometimes, I think I hear Him say to me, "Teri, is this thing on??" Then I realize I've been holding a very one-sided conversation. He desperately wants to give us His knowledge and wisdom. We just need to be still enough to hear Him.

Be silent, and know that I am God!   Psalm 46:10a NLT

This was the main reason Jesus went alone to pray. He didn't want to be distracted from hearing God. Jesus knew the best way to hear God's voice was to spend time alone with Him away from the whirlwind of life. This same practice can be applied to all of our relationships. How much does a relationship flourish when you spend quality time alone with each other? The best conversations are one-on-one discussions with no interruptions. The most peace-filled, surrendered people I know are people who spend the most amount of time alone, undistracted, conversing with their Father. One of my dearest friends, a spirit-filled lady that I greatly admire, can't exist without her hour each morning in devotions with her Lord.

Hard as I've tried, I can't get an extra hour into my daily routine. I have to "steal" moments with God several times a day. My best alone time with God is in the shower. It's pure heaven for 15 minutes each morning. For some reason I hear and pray clearly while I'm in there. I pray in the car while I'm waiting to pick up my daughter from school. I meditate while I'm walking. Any time I have to myself, I take it. Throughout my day, I might get an hour alone with Him, but I have to take it in smaller increments. There will be a season of my life after kids are grown and life isn't such a whirlwind, that I will have longer periods of alone time with God. But, for now, I take anything I can get. What's important is to make sure it's quality time spent with Him without allowing the distractions of life to get in the way.

On a Horse With No Name

"In the desert, you can remember your name
'Cause there ain't no one for to give ya no pain..." *Dewey Bunnell*

Since I don't get long periods of alone time with God, I've started taking "desert time." Once or twice a year, I try to get away from it all and spend a full day simply focusing on God. I've found my relationship deepens by taking these sabbaticals throughout the year. I call it, "a wander in the desert." When I'm feeling overwhelmed, tired and run down, I know it's been too long since my last "wander." My family knows that one to two times a year, I need to retreat somewhere alone without distractions. God usually provides somewhere for me to go for a day or two.

During that time, I remove any distraction except for my Bible, a reference book or two, my journal and music. As you can imagine, the first hour or so is torture. It is so hard to "unplug" and force my mind to be still. After I battle through for awhile, I finally allow God to fill all my thoughts.

40

Soon, the time flies by and it is time to go home completely filled, fueled and fired up once again.

PRAY UNCEASINGLY

We build our relationship with God by spending quality, uninterrupted time alone with Him. But, we also build a strong relationship by quantity prayer time with Him. We need to be praying to Him every moment we are awake. Think of it as one long, on-going conversation. No matter where we are or who is around, we can be talking with Him, contemplating His promises, praising Him. We can ask for His wisdom and guidance in the big things that impact our lives, or the seemingly meaningless stuff throughout our entire day. He wants all of us at all times.

Jesus told them a story showing that it was necessary for them to pray consistently and never quit.   *Luke 18:1 The Message*

I've learned, through much trial and error, to present my thoughts as prayers to God. For the most part, the thoughts whizzing around in my brain are developed as a conversation with my Father. If anyone could actually hear what goes on inside me, they would be rolling on the floor with laughter! I'm sure God has a chuckle Himself.

God's Snooze Button

Here is an example of how a typical morning conversation goes: "Good morning, Lord. WOW! Am I feeling old today. I don't really want to get out of bed. But, it is time unless the alarm clock got accidentally changed. Maybe You could just move time back one hour for me? Just one more hour? No? Okay. Please give me the strength to meet the demands of the day while I still focus on what you are doing in my life."

Your prayers don't have to be anything but rambling thoughts. We can pray while we are in the shower, driving to work, discussing politics, working on a project, serving in a ministry at church, having a conflict with our children, or reading a book. You don't need to pray aloud, bow your head, or kneel to be in prayer. We can focus on God throughout our day and fill our thoughts with Him no matter what we're doing.

Talking God's Lingo

When your children become teenagers, you suddenly start speaking different languages, or at least it seems that way to me. Now that I have teenagers, I know how easily misunderstandings can happen. Sometimes I feel like my kids and I *are* talking different language. I've realized how important it is to be in constant prayer asking God for help when I'm interacting with them. "Lord, I allow you to work through me so that when they look at me, they see you. Please give me your wisdom to handle this situation. Let Your love overflow to them. Your will be done!" I'm usually praying in my heart, the whole time I'm conversing. I want to make sure that the words falling from my lips are godly and encouraging.

I'm learning to see every interaction with others as an opportunity to shine Christ's love toward them. The only way I can be sure it's Christ and not me talking is to cover the interaction in prayer asking God to take over. "Lord, what do You want to do through this relationship? I relinquish my control and I will do or say whatever You ask of me."

When my heart is at that place, totally surrendered and willing, my relationships thrive because God is at the center of them. I can love others as Christ loves me, but only by His love overflowing from within me. Somehow, God fills me with just the right words at just the right time.

When we have surrendered ourselves to Christ, we realize that our lives revolve around Him. We need a strong relationship with Him to keep that in perspective. We need consistent quality and quantity prayer time with Him to make it grow, otherwise, we easily forget who is leading and allow our humanness to take control.

Since you have been raised to new life with Christ, set your sights on the realities of Heaven, where Christ sits at God's right hand in the place of honor and power. Let Heaven fill your thoughts. Do not think only about things down here on earth. Colossians 3:1-2 NLT

ENGAGING THE HOLY SPIRIT

Prayer is the best way for us to engage the Holy Spirit. The Holy Spirit is God's voice to us. His words and thoughts are communicated to us through His Spirit living within us. The more often we pray and listen, the more "in-tune" with the Holy Spirit we become. Jesus was so in-tune with the Holy Spirit He knew at all times and in all situations just the right words to use, the right locations to go, the right people to talk to and the right things to avoid. He said it was like He could "see" the Father doing it. He and His Father were one through the Holy Spirit.

Jesus gave them this answer: "I tell you the truth, the Son can do nothing by Himself; He can do only what He sees His Father doing, because whatever the Father does the Son also does.

John 5: 19 NIV

The Truth and Nothing But the Truth

God has written the truth deep within our spirits. All we ever need to know is there. Once we become a Christian, we are complete. We are whole. We have nothing lacking. God completed His work in us within our spirit. He is there whispering to us all we would ever need to know. The truth is planted within us and He wants us to be in-tune.

God has made everything beautiful for its own time. He has planted eternity in the human heart, but even so, people cannot see the whole scope of God's work from beginning to end.

Ecclesiastes 3:11 NLT

God knew we would struggle with understanding this truth. He knew we would still look outside of ourselves for truth. So He asked us to be in community with other believers. They can pray for us when we can't pray for ourselves. He can also use other Christians who give us morsels of His truth to help guide us.

Some of my most powerful answers to prayer have come to me through friends who are in-tune with the spirit within their heart. It is as if Jesus Himself is there telling me what He would have me know using their mouth as His instrument.

Don't miss out on that miracle. Make sure you're building strong relationships with other believers. Join a small group Bible study. Find a mentor. Get yourself an accountability partner who loves you enough to hold you accountable for your Christian journey. Network with other people who share similar situations. Open yourself up to others and risk being vulnerable. Push yourself out of your comfort zone and start growing closer to other Christians. God will be able to work in and through those relationships. Seek out the Holy Spirit in your prayer life and listen for His call.

The "Ear Wax" Waltz

What if you do all of these things and you still can't hear Him? Well, there is probably one of two things happening. Either you have something in the way that you need to remove like a little wax in the ear, or He is giving you a little space to allow you to grow.

Search your heart. Is there something gnawing at you from deep within? Do you have someone you need to forgive? Is there a conflict you have not resolved? Are you sinning in some area of your life which you have not given up yet? Are you being faithful to your family and to God? If something is triggering inside of you right now, don't ignore it. God could be revealing to you what is keeping you from hearing His voice. Ask God for clarity. If it is truly something God is asking you to deal with, embrace it. Celebrate God for revealing any garbage He wants you to let go. How quickly you get back on track is totally dependant on how willing you are to follow Him. Are you going to be hot or cold?

Sometimes we can't hear Him simply because He's stepped away from the microphone a little. He isn't ignoring you. He wants you to grow in your faith. He wants your faith to carry you forward. All we can do at that point is continue on the same path we've been traveling. Stay faithful, keep focused and keep surrendering. Soon, He will respond again and you will be blessed for your obedience.

Many times in my walk with Christ, I felt He had stepped away from the microphone. It felt like it was at exactly the wrong moment. But, for God, it was the perfect moment. He knew the precise time He needed to be still to give me the space I needed to grow in faith. With hindsight, now I see that it was indeed the perfect timing. Any moment sooner or later, and my faith wouldn't have grown as it did.

Then Jesus told him, "Because you have seen me, you have believed; blessed are those who have not seen and yet have believed."
John 20:25-30 NIV

EXPECT WONDERFUL THINGS

It is evident God has placed great importance on prayer by simply looking at references throughout the Bible. I encourage you to look up prayer in the concordance of your Bible and spend some time reflecting. Here are just a few of the references you will find:

I love the LORD because He hears and answers my prayers. Because He bends down and listens, I will pray as long as I have breath!
Psalm 116:1-2 NLT

44

On the day I called, You answered me; You made me bold with strength in my soul.   *Psalm 138:3 NASB*

Be joyful in hope, patient in affliction, faithful in prayer.
                                                   Romans 12:12 NIV

The prayer of a person living right with God is something powerful to be reckoned with.   *James 5:16b The Message*

There is no denying that prayer is critical for a healthy relationship with God. As if we need more incentive, He shows us time and time again that His children pray and He answers them.

- Abram prays for a son. (Genesis 15)
- Moses prays for a miracle at the red sea. (Exodus 14)
- Samson begs for the strength to bring the pillars down. (Judges 16:28-30)
- Solomon asks for wisdom. (1 Kings 3:1-15)
- Elijah pleads for rain. (1 Kings 18:41-46)
- Jabez asks to be blessed indeed. (1 Chronicles 4:9-10)

He is true to His word and He does listen and answer our prayers.

How Good and Pleasant!

We should spend prayer time with Him especially when we are distraught, confused or in turmoil. That is the time we should seek Him out without distractions as Jesus did in the garden. However, it seems to be the first thing that falls off the to-do list when life becomes chaotic.

Whether in our normal daily lives or when we are in turmoil, talking with our Father is essential to our surrender. How can we surrender to the One who is leading us, if we don't really know who He is? We can't. We will continue to fill ourselves with our own thoughts and desires and ignore what His Spirit is trying to communicate. Don't let that happen. Make a commitment today to spend time listening for His answer.

When you go to the Father in honest prayer, you can expect wonderful things. God hears us. God responds. God answers in miraculous ways. The more we practice, the more in-tune we become with the Holy Spirit's leadings. Our relationship with God and with others ignites when we have a prayer life that is aflame! Why hesitate to take everything to your loving Father, moment-by-moment conversing with Him?

Trust GOD from the bottom of your heart; don't try to figure out everything on your own. Listen for GOD's voice in everything you do, everywhere you go; He's the one who will keep you on track.

Proverbs 3:5-6 The Message

Questions to ponder:

1. Think about a time in your life that you felt closest to God. How was your prayer life during that time?

2. What are the barriers you experience in your prayer life? What are some ways you could overcome them?

3. Why is prayer important in your interactions with others?

4. How do you get "in-tune" with the Holy Spirit? Why is that important?

CHAPTER FIVE

DROP YOUR
NETS AND
FOLLOW ME

...there is a God present who at that very moment takes possession of
you. You may not feel it... but God takes possession if you will trust
Him. When God has begun the work of absolute surrender in you, and
when God has accepted your surrender, then God holds Himself bound
to care for it and to keep it. Will you believe that?
Andrew Murray

There is no fooling you, so I won't even try. This is the hardest step of the process. It requires self-reflection, honesty, vulnerability, courage and persistence. Many times we give up before we even get started. Just the thought of looking deep within our hearts is enough to scare us away.

There is no need to be afraid, instead, be encouraged! Once again, God comes through in miraculous ways to help us. He will be there to give us the strength we need. He takes possession of you and has bound Himself to the promise of caring for you. Nothing can harm us when He's on the job. He has given us a beautiful promise of freedom if we are willing take the step of faith and surrender.

You have died with Christ, and He has set you free from the evil powers
of this world. *Colossians 2:20a NLT*

Knowing we have a God-sized safety net around us makes this step easier. So, let's take a deep breath and step into the reality zone of honest self-reflection. The first step in self-reflection is to examine what it means to be human.

We need to first look at what God intended us to be when He created humans. Then, we need to understand what happened when Adam and Eve sinned and humans were cursed. We see the "before" and the "after" of humankind. We can then compare and contrast where we are today and get an honest picture of ourselves.

You might be thinking, "That's a strong dose of reality!" Yes, but never forget that God already sees reality very clearly. Yet, He still loves us with more passion than can be describes. He's not taken back by what He sees. He's still longing for a deeper relationship with us. He still wants to use us to further His plan. He's not afraid of reality.

We don't need to be afraid of reality either. We can stick it out and honestly assess all three aspects of our humanness; what we were created to be, what we became after the fall, and where we personally at today. When we do this, we "get real" with ourselves. God can use "real" people. He specializes in the "regular Joes." God knows that His truth will free us from our human bondage and transform us into something extraordinary.

Then you will know the truth, and the truth will set you free.
John 8:32 NIV

There is a great danger in not getting real. Satan can use people who would rather pretend. We become slaves to what we are hiding or hiding from. Satan hates it when we expose our hearts to God's light. Satan can no longer use the dark to shield his intentions from us. He has to come out of hiding. He can no longer subtly maneuver us into position. When we do a personal reality-check, Satan begins to shake with fear. It means that you are that much closer to dropping your nets and pursuing Christ with a heart on fire. He knows that when this happens, he won't be able to hold us captive to a lie any longer.

There are three parts to our personal reality check. To be successful in surrendering our humanness, we must fully understand all three aspects:

- What were humans created to be in the Garden of Eden?
- What happened to humans because of the fall?
- What is happening within our own heart today?

IN THE GARDEN OF EDEN

When God created Adam and Eve, He had wonderful things in mind for them. God envisioned a rich, full life for Adam without fear, resentment or shame – a world where human desires were pure and uncorrupted. He drew both of them close to Him and spoke with them regularly. He gave them authority, privilege and honor. God wanted only what was best for His children, so He gave us the greatest gift – Himself.

So God created man in His own image; in the image of God He created him; male and female He created them.   Genesis 1:27 NKJV

God only asked one thing from them in return. He made it very simple with only one rule. He asked them to surrender to His will and not eat of the fruit that would open their eyes to evil. They already knew goodness – they just didn't know evil. God knew that if they took the fruit, they would understand evil, temptation and impurity. He knew that this would eventually lead to sin and destruction. So, He asked Adam and Eve to trust Him and leave it alone.

That Nasty Little Liar

Satan manipulated the truth to make it seem that the reason God didn't want them eating the fruit was because He was somehow trying to stay superior. Can't you just imagine how Satan twisted the truth around? "God lied. If you eat this fruit, your eyes will be opened to the truth. That's why He has forbidden you to eat it. He's scared!"

The serpent tricked them into believing that they didn't already know goodness. If they had realized this, they probably would have made a better choice. The conscious decision-making process might have gone differently. "Ok, so I already know goodness and, boy is it good. But, I don't know evil. Is disobeying God worth knowing evil? Hummmm.... I think not!" Instead, they chose to distrust God and believe the lie that they would become just like God simply by eating this fruit. They chose to take matters into their own hands. They chose against God. They believed the lie that Satan spun.

The truth is that no matter what they did, they couldn't be like God. God knew this, Satan knew this, Adam and Eve knew this in their heart. The only option God gave Adam and Eve was to follow Him or not. The parents of humanity fell into the trap of being distracted from the simplicity God offers us.

Where's That Fig Leaf?

We suffer from the same problem today, God created the world to give us everything we could need. He provides for us. He knows what it will take to keep us safe from evil. He clothes us in His love and protection. He has very simple expectations of us. That's His plan and it's the only way we can truly be filled.

Satan comes around, whispering subtle lies to us which distort God's motivation. Satan tricks us into knowing evil. He beguiles us with false promises of greener pastures. Our discontented hearts eagerly follow in hopes of more to fill us. Once we accept Satan's lure, we find ourselves alone and naked – hiding behind our man-made cover-ups.

God cannot allow evil into His presence. His holiness would be tainted if sin were allowed in the garden, so must banish His beloveds from the place designed to supply all their needs. Now, they must toil and suffer. They are exiled from paradise.

So the LORD God banished him from the Garden of Eden to work the ground from which he had been taken.   Genesis 3:23 NIV

FALLEN FLESH

When Adam and Eve sinned, they were removed from God's presence. Everyone born of their seed is also separated from God. The consequence from their original sin is that we are born enemies of God – tainted at birth. We cannot escape our fallen flesh. We carry it with us each day as we walk around in these earthly bodies.

When Adam sinned, sin entered the entire human race. Adam's sin brought death, so death spread to everyone, for everyone sinned.
     Romans 5:12 NLT

There is nothing in our earthly flesh we can do to change our inheritance. There is no action or great work we can do on our own which will "untaint" us. We can never be good, do good, or represent good. We can never be holy enough to be in the presence of God. No other tainted flesh can lay hands on us, pray over us or anoint us to make us holy. Unless God steps in to transform us, we are all going to die and spend eternity separated from God. Nothing we could be or do would change that fact, ever.

Ewuoooo! That's Gross!

In John Marquez's book, *The Christ-Life Solution, 'It is Finished!'*, he paints an unattractive picture of fallen flesh. He describes it like meat, once fresh and good (as in the Garden), then left out of refrigeration for weeks. There is nothing that can be done to make it good again (as with fallen flesh). Nothing can cover the stench. It's rotten through and through. You can cook it, bake it, fry it, mix it in with fresh meat, but you still get the same result – spoiled meat. Only maggots seem to be able to enjoy it.[1]

It's enough to spoil your lunch! It's doubtful anyone wants to think of themselves as maggot-ridden rotten meat. However, it helps us realize that we can never be in God's presence in our fallen state.

OUR HOPE

Boy, that's enough to make you want to crawl into a hole and not come out! But, God isn't satisfied to leave it that way. He steps in and provides us hope! Our redeemer lived and died over two thousand years ago. Only by Christ's blood, His surrender upon the cross and victory in resurrection, can our spirits be transformed. Only then we are deemed holy enough to be reconciled to God. It is by God's power that we are healed. It was God's plan that Christ would take all of the responsibility for our salvation.

Salvation happens the moment we ask Christ to take over our life. Our spirits are instantly transformed and we become "new." The Holy Spirit enters and takes over. Where we were once dead, our spirits are now alive in Christ.

Therefore, if anyone is in Christ, he is a new creation; old things have passed away; behold, all things have become new.
2 Corinthians 5:17 NKJV

God created the plan for our salvation and Christ lived it out. Christ paid the penalty to pave the way back to a relationship with the Creator. Anyone who accepts this truth in their hearts is a new creation because of Jesus' ultimate surrender. Our sins are forgiven here on earth and we are assured a place in Heaven. We have hope for this life that carries on into eternity. An eternity spent with God.

He Gets the Job Done

So far we've seen how God created us in the Garden. He was to supply all of our needs. Then you see the devastation that happens when we all sin in our life; when we don't follow God. Then you see how God who loves us so completely that He offered His Son as the ultimate sacrifice to pay our debt. He did this so that we could be with Him again. Through Christ's death and resurrection, we have eternal life reconciled with our creator.

Up to this point, all the work has been done by God and God through Christ. But, He doesn't stop there. It's only the beginning of the incredible plan that God has for our lives. He carefully determined what resources, talents, gifts and situations we would need in order to embrace our new life. He knows just what events which need to take place in our lives in order to

PASSIONATE PEACE

prepare us for what lay ahead. He planned it all before time and is excited to see His dream fulfilled.

In this picture, it seems like there is a whole lot of God doing the work and very little responsibility left for us. BINGO! All He asks of fallen flesh is, you guessed it, surrender to His plan. He can use all we are and all we are not for His glory. God can use us even though we don't fully "get it" yet. He can use our successes and failures to further His plan. The surrender of our humanness is key to playing out this magnificent plan. Once we let go of the reigns, He can go to work.

FRAILTY OF LIFE

Another aspect to our humanness we inherited from Adam and Eve's sin is that our lives are short. Our lives are fleeting and frail. We cannot escape it. Our flesh is dying more each day.

> *How do you know what will happen tomorrow? For your life is like the morning fog – it's here a little while, then it's gone.*
>
> *James 4:14 NLT*

The fact that our lives are fleeting can be terrifying. It compels many people to live out their lives in fear and worry. They live as though they are in danger at every turn. They enslave themselves to the limits of potential consequences. Security is the god they seek above all others.

Because life is short, some people have chosen to live in the moment. They do as they please thinking little of the consequences. They are bound only by the limitations of what society will ultimately accept and the consequences of their actions. Pleasure is their primary goal.

Still, others are driven to achieve whatever they can get. "Whoever has the most toys wins!" Day in and day out their determination to gain all this life has to offer consumes them. They are confined to the limitations of their own capabilities. Success is their passion.

Empty Me of Me

I would venture to guess that each of us has wrestled with one or more of these issues at some point in our lives. We may still be resisting letting go of these goals. The only goal which will fill our needs is the pursuit of God. That is our purpose. When we empty ourselves of our humanness, we allow Christ to fill the void. Christ came so that we can live this life in fullness through Him.

The thief comes only to steal and kill and destroy; I came that they may have life, and have it abundantly. John 10:10 NASB

He wants our only limitation to be eternity.

Now glory be to God! By His mighty power at work within us, He is able to accomplish infinitely more than we could ever dare to ask or hope. Ephesians 3:20 NLT

I don't know about you, but I can imagine a lot! Yet, what seems to happen is nothing like I imagined it. Somehow it's better. Somehow, by following God each day (most days), I've ended up in a much different place. However, it is richer, fuller and deeper than I can explain. Funny how that happens. Looking back, I can see how God directed me here or there. But, it doesn't seem like I had much to do with it. He has accomplished more through my surrender than I could have ever dreamed. I'm excited to see where else He will lead.

Where's My Crystal Ball?

God has "eternal eyes". He asks us to hold tightly to the truth that He has a bigger and broader plan than our feeble eyes can see. This plan has nothing to do with our security, pleasure or success as viewed through the "worldly eyes" we were born with. Even in the midst of turmoil, we can choose to view our situation differently. God has the ultimate crystal ball. The Apostle Paul was great at seeing things differently than most humans. I love reading his books because he was an eternal optimist who had trained himself to see through "eternal eyes."

Therefore we do not lose heart. Though outwardly we are wasting away, yet inwardly we are being renewed day by day. For our light and momentary troubles are achieving for us an eternal glory that far outweighs them all. 2 Corinthians 4:16-17 NIV

In essence, Paul is saying, "I willingly empty myself of everything I am today for the hope of what God will do through me." He knew his life on earth was like a wisp of smoke that would soon vanish. He also knew the responsibility for knowing what to do, where to go and how to get there was already taken care of. God had him covered!

HONEST PERSONAL ASSESSMENT

Now that we understand what it means to be human and how God is there for us at every turn of our lives, we need to trust Him again as we look within ourselves. It's time for that personal reality check. We need to expose our inner-most desires, thoughts, perceptions and motivations. We need to stand before the mirror and take a good, long, honest look. When fallen flesh stands in the light of truth and gazes upon it's reflection in the mirror of righteousness we can see ourselves much more clearly. Nothing escapes the light of truth, especially in front of a righteous mirror.

Nothing in all creation can hide from Him. Naked and exposed before His eyes. This is the God to whom we must explain all that we have done. *Hebrews 4:13 NLT*

Stripping down to our naked human core and standing there exposed is never easy. Putting our heart under close scrutiny, we see the bruises and scars left from abuse, the tell-tale signs of neglect, the dark spots of unrepented sin, the weight of our indulgences and the weak areas of our personal limitations.

We might find memories filled with images of lust and pride. We could find ugly thoughts of revenge and scheming for our own gain. We have used our minds to think of getting more because we aren't content with what we already have. Our minds can be filled with self-doubt, worry and fear. Our insecurities can become so real they render our God-given abilities and talents useless.

The Air-Brush Defense

Since it is usually not a pleasant experience to take an honest look at our fallen flesh, humans have developed strong defense mechanisms. Remember the "programmed responses" that are at work within our hearts? They greatly impact the way we treat ourselves and others. A natural response to the ugliness within our core is to use this programming to distort reality. When we don't like the picture, humans will tend to view it differently. We like to take the "air-brushed" approach.

Let's say within your human core you feel like an insecure, wounded child. So, most of your behavior reflects that immaturity. But, when you look in the mirror, your binary code distorts this reality. Instead, you are programmed to see a determined, strong executive who has it all "put together." You use the air-brush to fill in what's lacking and smooth the rough edges. It softens the harsh reality. We work hard to keep the façade in place.

Or, you might see the opposite happening. You may have an extraordinary talent or gift that God is anxious to use. But because you can't believe you are "special," you distort your view and downplay your importance to God's plan. You are programmed to see an ordinary, boring individual who isn't special in any way. Our binary code can distort God's truth, just as an anorexic person can't see the thin person in the mirror. The distortion in our programming can help protect us from going outside our comfort zone. The air-brush is used to cover up what makes us uncomfortable, making it possible for us to live in denial.

The "If Only I Work Harder" Kung Fu

I know my battle all too well. It kept rearing its ugly head when I looked in the mirror. Just when I thought I had let it go, it came back. All my adult life I was driven to protect myself. I learned that through much self-discipline and perseverance, I could keep myself safe from most harm. If I worked-out and took good care of myself, stayed faithful in my Christian walk, followed the rules laid out before me and held my emotions in check – I would not get hurt. I also took it a step further. I thought that if I planned well enough, thinking through every contingency, I wouldn't get taken by surprise.

From the outside, I might have come off as solid, stable and secure. I've been told more than once, "You have your act together." I even began to believe it, that is, until the last couple of years. God has a way of breaking down our defenses even when we aren't aware they are there. I thought I was doing all the right things. However, I had left God out of the equation. I had forgotten that God protects me. I'm not super human. I don't have super human strength or abilities. My safety and security isn't my responsibility. That belongs to my creator.

Not that we are sufficient of ourselves to think of anything as being from ourselves, but our sufficiency is from God, who also made us sufficient as ministers of the new covenant, not of the letter but of the Spirit; for the letter kills, but the Spirit gives life. 2 Corinthians 3:5-6

Stuck Like a Pig at a Luau

So many people are stuck by either not wanting to see the reality of their sinfulness, or by only seeing the reality of their sinfulness. Of course, Satan is always there to help us stay stuck and continue to respond to life in the same empty way, over and over again.

If you are experiencing intense emotion right now, it's probably because you're stuck spiritually. Something, somewhere is holding you back. Some aspect of your humanness is too hard to let go. Have you been filled with guilt and shame but can't seem to get over it? Have you forgiven, truly forgiven, those who have hurt you? Have you forgiven yourself? Is there a secret you've been clinging to that needs to be revealed? What are the lies about yourself or others that you believe which keep you stuck?

Satan would have you stay on the rotisserie until you are cooked dry. However, God wants to heal you and quench your thirst.

When It's Too Hard

Often, breaking through the denial to the truth is too painful, too frightening, or too overwhelming. We don't want to "go there." We start down the path to reality only to quickly turn back and head for the safety of the air-brushed fantasy.

That is why so many of us tend to stop just before we fully face the mirror. Have you been there? Maybe you're there now? You feel as though it's a "catch-22" situation. If you stand in front of the mirror, you know you're going to see things you don't want to, but if you don't stand in front of the mirror those things will keep you stuck.

If it's too painful to admit it, we are reluctant to bring out in the open and ask for healing. So, we keep it locked away and the pain continues to fester and poison us. Pain and hurt left in our hearts over time produces anger, bitterness and fear. These are tools Satan uses to keep us from being healed. The more the pain grows, the more likely we won't surrender it, at least until much damage is done.

The same goes for guilt and shame. The more we hold on to them, the more powerful they become. Before long, the things we lock away and refuse to let go become overwhelming. At that point, we either "check-out" of our emotions or "bottom-out" emotionally and spiritually.

It is estimated that over 35 million Americans suffer from clinical depression at some point in their lives.[2] Over 14 million Americans are experiencing depression right now. How many do you think endure this pain because of locked away emotions left over time, festering in their heart? Only God knows for sure, but my guess is quite a few.

Our pain grows into fear which leads to guilt, which rots over time in our hearts, and ultimately can cause an emotional shut-down. This leads to a broken heart, which can only be healed by God's incredible love.

HE LOVES US IN OUR HUMANNESS

Jesus did not let His anguish stay locked away. He shared it immediately. He knew the damage that can be caused by holding on to it. Yet, HE DID NOT SIN. It doesn't say He was ashamed for His feelings – He openly admitted His sadness.

Then he said to them, "My soul is overwhelmed with sorrow to the point of death. Stay here and keep watch with me." Matthew 26:38 NIV

He reached out to others and reached up to God for comfort. He pleaded for God to take it from Him, to release Him from it. Still, HE DID NOT SIN. He willingly gave His humanness to His Father. He never seemed ashamed of His frail emotions.

When you have the courage to look in the mirror and "get real" with what's going on within you, God will meet you there. He wants to mend your broken heart. He longs for you to come running to Him, throw yourself into His arms and expect healing. We can't find it within ourselves, but He can provide the way. He tells us time and time again, we can trust Him.

And we know that God causes all things to work together for good to those who love God, to those who are called according to His purpose. Romans 8:28 NASB

"But, But, But..."

"But," you say, "we are fallen flesh, tainted at birth. Our flesh dies a little more each day. We get tempted and distracted with worldly things. What could God possibly see in us? How could God love such feeble creatures? I can't believe it!"

This is one of those areas where faith is needed. Some days we may know within the inner core of our being that God loves us beyond reason. Those are the good days. Some days we may only be able to tell ourselves, "I know God loves me beyond reason, even though I do not feel it right now." Those are the days we may struggle. Regardless of our thoughts or feelings, God's love for us never changes.

You saw me before I was born. Every day of my life was recorded in your book. Every moment was laid out before a single day had passed. How precious are your thoughts about me, O God! They are

innumerable! I can't even count them; they outnumber the grains of
sand! And when I wake up in the morning, you are still with me!
Psalm 139: 16-18 NLT

Have you tried to count the grains of sand in a square inch of beach,
much less all the sand in the world? Did you happen to count how many
exclamation points were used in this verse? After each sentence! God
wanted these words punctuated! God delights in you! He is concerned
with every aspect of you! He created you with great precision in perfect
harmony with the plan He has for you! Will you believe it?

THE BATTLE RAGES

Why is it so hard to believe? Why do we stumble? Why do we find it so
difficult to surrender ourselves? It's simple – we are at war. Each day there
is a battle raging in our hearts. More to the point, there is a battle raging
over our hearts. Do you feel it? Satan wants to continually remind us that
we are fallen flesh; weak and frail. He wants to pound the nail of
hopelessness so deeply into us that we never fully realize God's plan for
our lives. Satan lies and manipulates us into the stale living that comes
from denial and distortion.

If Satan cannot stop us from giving our lives to Christ, he can surely try
to stop us from realizing God's truth. Satan plays on the fact that we
haven't yet fully realized that our spirits are reborn. He banks on us being
afraid to "get real" with our human core. He counts on us to allow our lives
to become a whirlwind of activity which keeps us distracted. These are
Satan's tools.

He can't steal our freedom, but Satan can make us believe we are still
enslaved. The truth is we are now spiritually dead to sin by Christ's blood.
Satan wants to hide that truth from us. His only power is making us
believe his lies and neglect the truth.

From now on, think of it this way: Sin speaks a dead language that
means nothing to you; God speaks your mother tongue, and you hang on
every word. You are dead to sin and alive to God. That's what Jesus did.
Romans 6:11 The Message

Freedom comes only when we take each lie we have believed and
surrender it to God in prayer. We then allow Him to replace it with the
truth as we listen for His response. In the Garden of Eden, Adam and Eve

believed Satan's distorted reality. In the Garden of Gethsemane, Christ replaced the lies with truth. Which garden do you choose?

Reality TV Done God's Way

In the Bible, we find numerous examples of godly people who had obstacles to giving all of themselves to God. Some of these people were able to surrender their weaknesses so God could use them. Others got "stuck" and allowed Satan to use them. Here is a short list of people who have appeared in God's reality show and the obstacles making them resist God's truth:

- Adam and Eve – Lacked trust and courage. Adam's insecurity made him too weak to resist the temptation. Eve couldn't trust God's faithfulness. (Genesis 3)

- Saul – Saul's pride was so strong it hardened his heart so that God ultimately turned away from him. (1 Samuel 15)

- David – David lacked the self-discipline needed to resist temptation. His lust drove him to adultery and murder. (2 Samuel 11-12)

- Esther – Esther's fear almost kept her from saving her nation. (Esther 4-7)

- Solomon – Solomon was driven to try everything available to him to fill him. His lack of contentment kept him looking everywhere else but to God. (Ecclesiastes)

- Job – Job's despair was almost his undoing. He almost lost himself to grief. (Job)

- Peter – Peter's fear compelled him to betray his Lord. At first, he was not willing to risk personal injury for what he believed. (John 18:15-27)

God can use our humanness in spite of ourselves to further His plan if we let Him. We can also see the consequences of controlling our own outcomes. What a glorious proposition it is to "drop our nets" and allow God to work His miracles!

Pace Yourself
There is a rhythm and flow to this step. If we dwell too long on our human frailties and let them become our focus, we give them too much power. It allows Satan a foothold to plant seeds of fear, discontent and turmoil. Satan revels in pointing out our weaknesses. He rejoices when we feel powerless over temptation. When we feel defeated or scared to move forward, we know that Satan is trying to hold us hostage to our humanness. This is the signal that it's time to move on to step three, Know God.

On the other hand, if we don't spend enough time honestly assessing ourselves and try to move on to step three too quickly, God lovingly brings us back to examine what we missed. Sometimes He reminds us gently, and sometimes the most loving thing to do is to hit us with the "truth hammer". He's had to pound some sense into me more than once. No matter how He guides you, it is always just what you need when you need it. He doesn't want anything to get in the way of working out His plan.

Therefore, since we are surrounded by such a huge crowd of witnesses to the life of faith, let us strip off every weight that slows us down, especially the sin that so easily hinders our progress. And let us run with endurance the race that God has set before us.
Hebrews 12:1 NLT

Either way, we must learn to recognize the signs of moving too slowly or quickly. There is great benefit in going through the steps at the right pace.

WHAT ARE YOU CLINGING TO?

What is holding you back from taking that next step to fulfill God's plan? What areas of your life do you resist to let go? What do you have your fingers curled tightly around? What are you fishing for that you don't think you can find by following Christ?

In Jesus' situation, it was very obvious. Pain, suffering, humiliation and separation from God would make anyone sweat drops of blood. Your situation might be more subtle. Past hurts might be keeping you from forgiveness and healing. You might be experiencing obstacles beyond your control which affect you. You might be dealing with consequences of your past sins. God can work through whatever comes your way. He has you covered no matter what!

No temptation has overtaken you except such as is common to man; but God is faithful, who will not allow you to be tempted beyond what you

are able, but with the temptation will also make the way of escape, that
you may be able to bear it.   *1 Corinthians 10:13 NKJV*

Make a list of every obstacle you can think of that is keeping you from surrendering to God. Are you afraid, ashamed, confused, angry, resentful, or disappointed? What is at the route of your feelings? Why do you battle with letting them go? Take a long, hard look at where your feelings are coming from. Give yourself a personal reality-check and then take everything to your Father in prayer. Ask Him to forgive and heal you. Ask Him to help you work through whatever holds you back and He will come through. His promises are true.

God Is Bigger Than All That

Whether your obstacle is emotional, physical, mental, financial or something else, it needs to be honestly acknowledged. We must scrutinize our humanness in front of the mirror of righteousness. We need to "get real" and openly admit our shortcomings. Then we must choose to follow God even though these obstacles exist, even though we may not feel like taking another step. Go on anyway. God will meet you there. You can look in the mirror and honestly bring yourself before God even though you are flawed. It's what He wants – it's what He asks us to do. It's the second step toward surrender.

The more we willingly give of ourselves to God, the more He reveals who He created us to be. As you empty yourself of your humanness, the Christ within you shines through. The transformation is a beautiful process to behold. Our responsibility is to "get real" with our humanness and turn it over to God. Then He comes through in miraculous ways to bestow His reality on us. He transforms:

- Worldly eyes into eternal eyes
- Shame into freedom
- Fear into power
- Despair into peace
- Resentment into forgiveness
- Complacency into vitality

Recklessly abandon whatever you're clinging to and feel His love miraculously transform you.

To those who have sorrow in Zion I will give them a crown of beauty instead of ashes. I will give them the oil of joy instead of sorrow, and a spirit of praise instead of a spirit of no hope. Then they will be called oaks that are right with God, planted by the Lord, that He may be honored.

Isaiah 61:3 NLV

Questions to Ponder:

1. Why does God ask us to look honestly at our humanness?

2. How can God still love us even with our imperfections? Do you believe this deep within your heart?

3. What "nets" do you need to abandon so you can follow Christ more passionately?

CHAPTER SIX

KNOW
GOD

"We cannot but admit that not even the least thing takes place unless it is ordered by God. For who have ever been so concerned and curious as to find out how much hair he has on his head? There is no one. God, however, knows the number. Indeed, nothing is too small in us or in any other creature, not to be ordered by the all-knowing and all-powerful providence of God." Huldrych Zwingli

Then Moses said, "I pray You, show me Your glory!" And He said, "I Myself will make all My goodness pass before you, and will proclaim the name of the Lord before you...But He said, "You cannot see My face, for no man can see Me and live!"

Then the LORD said, "Behold, there is a place by Me, and you shall stand there on the rock; and it will come about, while My glory is passing by, that I will put you in the cleft of the rock and cover you with My hand until I have passed by.

"Then I will take My hand away and you shall see My back, but My face shall not be seen."   *Exodus 33:18-19-23 NASB*

This scripture keeps going through my head as I start to write this chapter. No man on earth can see God and live. How could I possibly describe something so awesome and limitless? There have been thousands of books written about God. Each one has failed to describe Him in His fullness. I find myself lost as to how to even begin. How can you possibly know God? Well, this is where we take a deep breath and start from the beginning. Let's start with what we do know.

We know that we serve a mighty God; the Alpha and Omega, the Beginning and the End, the I Am. We serve the One who is too large to name. No single name fits Him. The Bible only uses titles and words to describe Him and is never able to give Him a name. Here are a few of the names given to Him in the Bible and their meanings:

- El Shaddai – God almighty, or all sufficient
- Adonai – Master
- Jehovah Elohim – Self-existent one
- Jehovah-Jireh – The Lord will provide
- Jehovah-Rophe – The Lord who heals
- Jehovah-M'Kaddesh – The Lord who sanctifies
- Jehovah-Shalom – The Lord our peace
- Jehovah-Sabaoth – The Lord of Hosts

He could fill a mountain top with His presence. He could take on flesh when needed or a burning bush if it suited Him, yet no one could look upon His magnificence without instant death. Moses was close to seeing Him in His full glory, and Moses had to look at Him from behind or through a burning bush. God is the creator of Heaven and earth. He is eternal, all-knowing, ever-present and pure love. He cannot lie and He cannot fail.

This, dear friends, is who we are surrendering to – one who is too large to name. We serve the One whose precious thoughts about us are more numerable than all the grains of sand. It tends to put our fear of surrendering our humanness into proper perspective. "Dropping our nets" becomes much less difficult once we have a realistic picture of the Master. He is absolutely, completely, utterly trustworthy.

After you've taken the difficult step to realistically view your humanity, gazing upon God's majesty is breathtaking! He is the God who wants to give us beauty for ashes (Isaiah 61:3). He lovingly, painstakingly created an incredible plan for each of us which is more than we could ever dare ask or imagine (Ephesians 3:20). All that He is remains a mystery to us. Yet, He longs for us to get to know Him better.

HIS AWESOMENESS

How do you get to know Him better? There are many things about Him that we may never fully understand; however, He gives us many glimpses into His character throughout the Bible. One of the best ways to get to know Him better is through a solid prayer life, which we've already talked about. Another avenue we have to know Him better is to study His Word. Here are a few things we know about Him through the Bible.

Creator of All Things

I was an atheist when I was a teenager and very actively spoke out against creation and any concept of an all-powerful God. It was too much for me to believe that life was more than what each person made of it.

C.S. Lewis also was once an atheist, who later became a Christian. After becoming a Christian, he wrote, "People who take that view [evolution] think that matter and space just happen to exist, and always have existed, nobody knows why; and that the matter, behaving in certain fixed ways, has just happened, by sort of a fluke, to produce creatures like ourselves who are able to think."

As an atheist, I was with him that far. I believed that life simply fell together in some primordial soup and over eons of time, evolved into what we are today. It seemed, at the time, an easier concept to believe than believing in God.

But, Mr. Lewis didn't stop there. He continued, "By one chance in a thousand something hit our sun and made it produce the planets; and by another thousandth chance the chemicals necessary for life, and the right temperature, occurred on one of these planets, and so some of the matter on this earth came alive; and then, by a very long series of chances, the living creatures developed into things like us." [3]

Well! Put it that way, and it makes you start thinking about how outrageous it sounds. Which is more outrageous? Believing there is a supernatural being that designed and created life? Or that somehow, some way all the right cosmic forces and basic components of life were perfectly set in motion to produce order from chaos?

As for my conversion from atheism to Christianity, I thank God He never gave up on me. He kept calling me until I finally heard Him. Eventually, I realized that deep within me I knew the truth of God's existence. Deep down, I knew that God created me. My atheism was just another way of keeping myself safe and trying to control my life.

He Is Eternal

The oldest person on record over the last few centuries lived to be around 115 years old. The oldest person recorded in the Bible lived to be over 900. While we may be able to comprehend living 115 years, 900 years on earth might be too much of a stretch for us. That is why it may be impossible for us to fully comprehend that God has neither beginning nor end. He cannot die. He is eternal. He is everlasting. He is infinite. The Bible doesn't tell us of God's origin nor does it tell us of His end.

> *Don't be afraid! I am the First and the Last. I am the living One who*
> *died. Look, I am alive, forever and ever! And I hold the keys of death*
> *and the grave.*   *Revelations 1: 17b-18 NLT*

No beginning; no end. He just IS. I am the I AM (Exodus 3:14). But, what does this mean to us? The One we serve does not fall victim to the sequence of time. He lives without limitations of the calendar. Humans cannot escape the ticking of the clock – but God can. He does not age and He will not die. He existed since the beginning of time and He will continue to be with us always. He is the one constant in time who holds all things together (Colossians 1:15-17).

He is All-Knowing

God is also not bound by sequential thinking. As we pondered how God could know everything, my mom often said, "He must have a very big computer." God knew the beginning from the end. He foresaw everything that would happen in our lifetimes and throughout history. There isn't one thing He isn't aware of. Not one thought, action or inaction, not one tear or moment of time happens without His knowledge.

He knew each of us before we were born. He has the number of hairs on your head counted. He knew what would happen to us and how we would live our lives. He knew what choices we would and wouldn't make. He knew what we would need in our life to help draw us to Him. He knew the times we would be tempted and what it would take to help us out. He knew just what it would take to get us to this point in our daily walk. This is how He has developed His plan. If hindsight is 20/20, then God's foreknowledge is better than the Hubble Telescope.

He has equipped each of us with everything we need to handle the troubles of today. He knew how to make us look, how to build our character and what talents and weaknesses we would need in order to fulfill His plan. He also knew when we would reject His plan and choose our own way. So, He even prepared a way that would allow Him to make our mistakes turn out for good.

He Is Ever-Present

God is not bound by sequential time, thinking or space. I have a body. I have form and mass. I am limited to being in one place at one time. Our human minds can barely fathom the thought of not being limited to a sequential timeline, much less understand the power needed to have omnipresence. Some days, it might be nice to be in more than one place at one time. But, being everywhere throughout history from the beginning of time to the end of time?

"...and lo, I am with you always, even to the end of the age." Amen.
Matthew28:20b NKJ

He's also present within us once we accept Him in our hearts. He's here, living within me and you. The Holy Spirit takes up residence in our spirit and connects all of us to God. We are all bound together in Him as branches in a vine.

I am the vine, you are the branches. He who abides in Me, and I in him, bears much fruit; for without Me you can do nothing.
John 15:5 NKJ

God's Holodeck

The best way for me to put my mind around God's power is to create an analogy. In the TV show, Star Trek the Next Generation, I always enjoyed watching the scenes played out on the holodeck. It was where the people of the 24th century went to have a little fun. It's a computerized super-room which displays a convincing land of make-believe. It's kind of like the cross between a movie, a reality show and video role-playing game.

There was one character, Data, who loved Sherlock Holmes. Data would input elements from the novels; Sherlock, Watson, Professor Moriarty, London, Baker Street, etc. He would give the computer all the information it needed in order to build a role-playing program. Somehow it magically put all the components together and came up with life-like scenes and realistic characters.

Once this was all done, Data would dress up like Sherlock Holmes, step into the Holodeck and play out a scene with the computer. There was no script; the flow was simply based on how the computer was programmed and Data's interaction. There would be a new mystery to be solved each time he stepped into the holodeck. The old characters would be there as well as new ones for Data to meet.

I wish I had a holodeck in my house. I'd devise a program of Lake Tahoe in the early summer. My program would have a beautiful log cabin with a breath-taking view overlooking the lake. The weather would always be perfect and the water would be warmer than what it truly is. I could retreat into my "vacation holodeck" whenever I got tired of the daily grind. What an invention that would be!

Let's imagine that God has a holodeck. It is a large round room made up of tons of computer sensors in the walls. All of the happenings throughout time, from before the earth was formed to the end of all time, are played on the walls of this room. He can see all of the images throughout history revealed to Him at the same time.

He can see every event in our lives simultaneously; past, present and future. Since He has already seen what we will do within certain situations, He knows what we will need in order to give us the opportunity to make the best choice. He has already been where we are; He's already walked in our steps. He knows what plan is needed for us to be successful in the life He wants for us.

Not only can He see all the images, He is present IN the images. As He watches from the holodeck, He is also experiencing the happenings. His spirit dwells everywhere. He is living out through me and you yesterday, today and tomorrow. *All at the same time!* He is working in the heart of someone else. He is there when Johnny falls down and hurts His knee. A sparrow falls and He is there too. Not being bound by sequential time or space is an incredible concept!

Another interesting aspect to this picture is that the images on the wall include not only the seen world, but the unseen world; the physical and the spiritual realms. God is aware of what all humans are doing – past, present and future. He is also attentive to what angels and demons are involved in. He is simply awesome.

He is the image of the invisible God, the firstborn over all creation. For by him all things were created: things in heaven and on earth, visible and invisible, whether thrones or powers or rulers or authorities; all things were created by him and for him. He is before all things, and in him all things hold together. *Colossians 1:15-17 NIV*

Ouch! I Think I Broke My Brain

I am really glad He's got it figured out, because my brain is starting to hurt from over exertion! Still, it comes down to faith. If we truly believe that God is as magnificent as the Bible tells us, then we rely on Him to fill in the details. Faith is what we must fall upon when our minds become too overwhelmed with concepts that are beyond our comprehension.

Many have grappled with this inability to fully understand God's magnificence. It has led many down the path of atheism or other beliefs because their minds could simply not believe such things are possible. No matter the argument, there seems to always be a counter-argument. We are dealing with matters much too enormous for even the sharpest intellects. God reminds us that we simply can't understand it all.

> *For My thoughts are not your thoughts, nor are your ways My ways,"*
> *declares the LORD.*   *Isaiah 55:8 NASB*

As if this wasn't incredible enough, He loves each one of us with more passion than we can comprehend.

HE IS LOVE

Ah, love! C'est manifique! His love is all-consuming. It's real and alive and it is available to anyone. How else could people be drawn toward Him 2,000 years after God in human flesh walked on earth? You can't define it; you can't prove it. You can only drink it in. Once you experience His unconditional love, you are never the same.

Everyone around Jesus was drawn to His love; whether they responded positively or negatively. The people who were empty and incomplete responded to Him with great passion. The ones who thought they had it all figured out with their rules and regulations tended to answer His love with anger and fear. They couldn't believe that anyone could be so loving. So, they concluded, He must be evil. This influence Jesus had over others terrified the people in power. Jesus led by example and love, not by intimidation and coercion. That kind of leadership can change the world, and it did.

That's Hollywood!

Our world today is almost devoid of real love. There's plenty of lust and infatuation. We see all kinds of whirlwind romances which fire off like a rocket and then burn out. We see loads of selfish love. There is an abundance of needy people who clinging to each other until they are both empty. Then they have to move on to someone else. "I love you because of what you do for me." "I can't live without you!" "I'm nothing without you!" This self-centered love might work great in the movies, but in real life it doesn't last. True love it self-less.

> *What a man desires is unfailing love...*   *Proverbs 19:22 NIV*

Any other kind of love is artificial and temporary. To love others as our self would suggest that we must first be able to love our self in a healthy way. I think one of the biggest problems we face today is people who don't love themselves, trying to love someone else. It just doesn't work.

How do we love ourselves? God helps us with that. He says we can love others because He has loved us. The love flows from Him. That is why He requires us to love Him above anything else. When we love Him with all our hearts, minds, and strength we open ourselves up for a "love download" of enormous proportions.

As the Father has loved me, so have I loved you. Now remain in my love.
John 15:9 NIV

I Think That Just About Covers It

I did a Bible study once which examined the following scripture to see if it left out any possible scenario. The enquiring minds in the class could not find one single aspect to human life which it didn't cover. We can never be separated from Christ's love.

For I am convinced that neither death, nor life, nor angels, nor principalities, nor things present, nor things to come, nor powers, nor height, nor depth, nor any other created thing, will be able to separate us from the love of God, which is in Christ Jesus our Lord.
Romans 8:38-39 NASB

Let that wash over you for a moment. Can you think of anything else on earth that is so totally encompassing? Why did Paul spend so much time and thought making sure he covered every conceivable situation? Because God wants us to believe it!

The only picture that comes remotely close is that of a parent toward a child. I know my mom and dad would do anything humanly possible for me without a second thought about themselves. They love me that much. I feel that way about my children. I can't think of one thing that would make me stop loving them. Most parents would even battle the powers of hell for the good of their children.

Even still, God loves us more than that. Nothing can separate us from this incredible love. So, we serve our creator who is eternal, all-knowing, ever-present, *AND* loves us beyond all comprehension.

It Just Pours Out

As we become filled with that love, it just naturally overflows to those around us. We will naturally start developing stronger, deeper relationships. We begin to see our unhealthy relationships and seek to grow healthy ones.

If you aren't experiencing unconditional love in your life, you aren't surrounding yourself with the right people. Everyone needs at least one person who loves them unconditionally. Not a perfect person, just someone who will love you no matter what. I'm blessed to have a lot of people in my life who love me without condition. Praise God!

Their love has greatly impacted my life. My close circle of loved ones gives me just what I need in order to stay strong in my relationship with God and the rest of the world. They inspire me and keep me going when I start feeling overcome with distractions. If I'm hurting, confused, or empty I go to God, and I can seek God through my loving friends and family. They are my "angels" on earth who minister to me.

This is how powerful God's love is. He lives within us so He can fill us and overflow to everyone around us. It's utterly amazing! His love is better than life itself.

HE IS TRUSTWORTHY

We've taken a look our awesome God. We know He loves us unconditionally. We now that He cannot lie. He cannot sin. He cannot fail. Otherwise, He couldn't be God. Therefore, He is totally, wholly and utterly trustworthy. He can't allow sin into His presence, so therefore, by His own nature, cannot be anything but completely trustworthy.

The Bible is full of God's promises and their fulfillment:

Know therefore that the LORD your God, He is God, the faithful God, who keeps His covenant and His lovingkindness to a thousandth generation with those who love Him and keep His commandments;
Deuteronomy 7:9 NASB

And the words of the LORD are flawless, like silver refined in a furnace of clay, purified seven times. *Psalm 12:6 NIV*

For the word of the LORD holds true, and everything he does is worthy of our trust. *Psalm 33:4 NLT*

Many of us have difficulty trusting Him; most likely because we've been hurt and betrayed enough to become distrusting. In the majority of the counseling sessions I take part in, distrusting God is at the root of most issues. People develop ways to protect themselves from pain and have deeply embedded them into their binary code. Now, they respond from the programming without recognizing why they behave the way they do.

If we haven't had many trustworthy people in our lives, it becomes nearly impossible for us to trust someone we have never seen. This world teaches us to believe only in what we can taste, touch, smell, hear and see. This gradual "brainwashing" effect can leave us vulnerable to our doubts.

I Trust God. Don't I?

Sometimes, we don't even realize we are neglecting to trust God. We can become habitually self-reliant. A few years back, if someone would have asked me if I trusted God, I would have determinedly said, "YES!" Then I would have gone about my day, working and striving to keep myself safe from harm, relying totally on myself to control my life. I didn't even realize I wasn't trusting God.

> *The fundamental fact of existence is that this trust in God, this faith, is the firm foundation under everything that makes life worth living. It's our handle on what we can't see.*   Hebrews 11:1 The Message

Have you been holding the control of your life back from God? What about in the area of your finances? This seems to be a big sticking point for trust. Do you ask, "Lord, how do you want me to use your money?" It is so easy to do what we've always done, spend what we always have, and forget to ask God for guidance. In any area of our life, if we are not depending on God's leadership, we are distrusting Him.

That Really Torks Me Off!

We can hold the reigns of control of our life in very subtle ways. We might manipulate our spouses, our children, our friends and co-workers for personal gain. Let's say your spouse has really upset you. They've done something that hurts you very deeply. It makes you feel like you can't trust them and deep down you may feel rejected. In this scenario, we might react either with anger and speak harshly, we might keep quiet and just fume, or we might try to manipulate with guilt or other techniques.

If we are really trusting God, our first choice is to take it to Him. "Lord, I'm upset. I'd really like to tell him/her off! It hurts me when he/she lets me down. I feel like everything else is more important to him/her than I am. I need your help. I know I can trust You in this matter. How would you have me respond? Should I confront him/her in love? Or should I forgive him/her and let it go? Either way, You are going to have to fill me with

Your love and help push out my resentment. I don't feel very loving toward him/her right now." Do you respond that way? If you are like 99% of the people in the world, the answer would be, "No!" The question should be, do you trust God to work it out or do you feel compelled to work it out on your own?

How about when you are driving and someone recklessly cuts you off? Do you mutter (or yell) nasty sentiments toward that person? You've probably done it at least once or twice. But, to fully trust God is to go to Him immediately. "That was so dangerous. It makes me so mad when people are that reckless – like they didn't even see me! Lord, I pray for her/his safety and the others on the road. Please work within their hearts to get them to slow down and be more careful. Thank you for protecting me."

Keeping It All in Perspective

An important thing to keep in mind is that our journey is not about being happy. That isn't the goal God has in mind. It's nice to be happy. We like it and it feels good. But, that's not what God is trying to accomplish. He wants us to grow and mature in our love for Him by unconditionally loving those He created. The deeper we grow in our relationship with Him and others, the more joy and peace we experience.

It helps me to remember that when we die, we will be alone when we meet Christ. When He greets us, He will not be concerned with what others did or didn't do to you, nor what they said or didn't say to you. Christ will only be concerned about what we did or didn't do, and what we said or didn't say. He will test our heart to see how we responded to only one question, "To what degree did we surrender to His leadership?"

Trust is a major ingredient in surrender. We must believe that God is trustworthy with everything; otherwise, we will continually resist giving our lives to Him. We can trust Him to help us respond to the world around us. We can trust Him to work in other people's heart without our manipulation or control. We can be honest with Him at all times with what we're thinking and feeling because He already knows us. That's the way Jesus responded to every moment on earth and His Spirit lives within you.

The "Fear Factor" Check-Up

Here is a quick self-test to see how deeply you believe God's love for you. Read the following scripture and rate yourself on a scale from 1-10. Rate yourself a one if you feel consumed by fear most of the time. Rate yourself a ten if you experience fear only if you get chased by a large, predatory animal.

We know it so well, we've embraced it heart and soul, this love that comes from God. God is love. When we take up permanent residence in a life of love, we live in God and God lives in us. There is no room in love for fear. Well-formed love banishes fear. Since fear is crippling, a fearful life--fear of death, fear of judgment--is one not yet fully formed in love.

1 John 4:16, 18 The Message

If you are experiencing worry, anger or bitterness, then there is probably fear in your life. These emotions are usually secondary reactions to fear. Somehow, someway you have not fully given yourself over to believing Christ's love for you. You don't think you can trust God completely.

Many times I hear people say, "I know how much God loves me." But, then the next words out of their mouth are filled with worry or resentment. It's time to do a check-up on your belief system. There is a lie you believe somewhere deep within your heart which needs to revealed. Ask God to reveal the truth to you and release you from the lie.

It won't happen over night. It is a growth process. His love gets perfected in us over time. The fear subsides as the more of ourselves we give to Christ. The more we live in God, the more He lives in us. After over 20 years of being a Christian, I'm just now starting to see the true nature of God. It's taken me this long to get to know Him and deeply feel His love for me, mainly because I doubted His love for me.

You Don't Know Anything, Dad!

When you have a better understanding of who God is, you begin to see a fuller picture of His perfect design for your life. You see why the only thing He expects from us is to surrender to His plan. He knows what is best for our lives. He asks that we follow the path He has laid before us. Yet, sometimes we still resist it.

I think of my dad and when I was a strong-willed teenager who knew everything. I remember the look on his face after I explained the true meaning of life according to Teri. He looked at me with great compassion, shook his head and said, "Some day, I hope you see things differently." He knew he wouldn't be able to argue me out of my position. I'd just have to learn and grow and find my own way. He also realized he'd have to be around to pick up the pieces when I fell flat on my face.

I imagine God shaking His head at us when we keep missing the point. Not out of judgment or condemnation, but out of love and compassion for us. "Well, my child. I'll still be here when you find out that path leads to no where." Now that I have teenagers of my own, I realize the wisdom of allowing them to find their own way when they don't necessarily make the best choices. I also know that God will light their path at just the precise moment they need it, just as He did for me.

THE MYSTERY

There is something deep inside each of us that longs to be reconciled with our loving creator. Many people feel that primeval call but never respond to it. Something in their human core can't allow them to "take the leap of faith." Sometimes, even after we take that leap, we can still have nagging doubts about the validity of all that God asks us to believe.

God created us to reason, to question and have doubt. He loved His disciple Thomas as much as He loved the others, even though Thomas was a very hard person to convince of supernatural things. Moses questioned and debated, and sometimes bargained with God. God came through each time to show Moses and Thomas that He was everything He claimed to be. If you have a hard time believing, go ahead and ask God to reveal Himself to you. Ask for a better understanding of His power. He will not disappoint.

Who is like You among the gods, O LORD? Who is like You, majestic in holiness, awesome in praises, working wonders?
Exodus 15:11 NASB

God is that big. Our doubts do not diminish anything about Him. He is immutable. He's not bound by time, thought or space. His is limitless and He longs for you to return His love. He wants to reveal Himself to you and help you grow in your understanding.

Those in Christ will spend eternity with Him in Heaven. Here on earth, getting to know Him is a little more difficult. Yet, once again, God has given us just what we need to help. We don't have to go far to get to know the God of the universe. He isn't some spirit sitting on a throne, gazing on us from a great distance. Christ isn't just walking beside us. He lives within us. Right here, right now. He is part of us and we are part of Him. We carry Him with us wherever we go; inseparable entities. When God looks at us, He sees Christ. Why? How? It's a mystery. It's time to embrace it with all of our heart. How better for us to get acquainted?

When I think of the wisdom and scope of God's plan, I fall to my knees and pray to the Father, the Creator of everything in Heaven and earth. I pray that from His glorious, unlimited resources He will give you mighty inner strength through His Holy Spirit.

And I pray that Christ will be more and more at home in your hearts as you trust in Him. May your roots go down deep into the soil of God's marvelous love. And may you have the power to understand, as all God's people should, how wide, how long, how high, and how deep His love really is.

May you experience the love of Christ, though it is so great you will never fully understand it. Then you will be filled with the fullness of life and power that comes from God.   *Ephesians 3:14-19 NLT*

Questions to ponder:

1. How would you describe God?

2. What doubts about God do you struggle with?

3. Why is God completely trustworthy?

4. What aspects of your life do you find it hard to trust God?

CHAPTER SEVEN

UNTIL YOU
HAVE PEACE

If our religion be of our own getting or making, it will perish; and the sooner it goes, the better; but if our religion is a matter of God's giving, we know that He shall never take back what He gives, and that, if He has commenced to work in us by His grace, He will never leave it unfinished.
Charles Spurgeon

I know what you might be saying, "Ok, so I've gone to my Father in prayer, I've surrendered my humanness to Him, and now I know God better. But, I still don't have peace." AH! Yes! But, there are four steps.

First, we must build a strong relationship with the Father through prayer. Quantity and quality time is important to grow in that relationship. Then we must honestly assess our heart; strip it down and look at it in front of the mirror of righteousness. When we have a realistic view of ourselves, we then must willingly surrender all that we are and all that we are not to Christ. We choose to drop our nets and relentlessly follow Him. To help us in this process, we need to get to know God better. The better we understand His character and trustworthiness, the easier it becomes to surrender ourselves to Him.

Now, we need to keep repeating these steps until we have peace. This last step typically gets ignored and often why we might fail at fully surrendering. If you have peace right now, rejoice and praise God for His blessing! If you don't have peace yet, don't give up! Try again. Persist in your pursuit. Remind yourself that it's not up to you. Trust God that He will help you find lasting peace. He has provided a fail-proof way to succeed at this step, too. We just need to stay in the race until it is finished.

I don't mean to say that I have already achieved these things or that I have already reached perfection! But I keep working toward the day

*when I will finally be all that Christ Jesus saved me for and wants me
to be.*   *Philippians 3:12 NLT*

As the truths about ourselves and God become clearer, surrender gradually becomes a habit. Repetition becomes the vehicle we use to engrain these truths deeply into our lives.

OUR TRANSFORMATION

Having to repeat the steps does not mean you have failed. That would be another lie of Satan – to trick you into feeling defeated and hopeless. NO! How does someone learn how to ride a bike? They learn by trying over and over again until they get better. They might fall several times at first, but gradually they learn to keep their balance.

Repetition is simply the way to getting the truth implanted deep into your core. It is what Paul calls, "renewing your mind" (Romans 12:2) and "putting on your new man" (Ephesians 4:24). We must change the way we think about ourselves and about God. We must reprogram ourselves by entrenching the truth into our hearts.

The transformation of our human core happens as we reprogram our minds to live by God's truths. In Romans, Paul pleads with us to open our minds to the higher truth that God gives us and not fall victim falseness of this world.

Therefore I urge you, brethren, by the mercies of God, to present your bodies a living and holy sacrifice, acceptable to God, which is your spiritual service of worship. And do not be conformed to this world, but be transformed by the renewing of your mind, so that you may prove what the will of God is, that which is good and acceptable and perfect.
Romans 12:1-2 NASB

This is a powerful scripture which teaches us how to surrender each day. When we renew our minds to the truth, we open the door to our hearts wider to God. We surrender our humanness to God and then He transforms us into new creations. His love growing within us can't help but overflow to the others around us. It's a perfect cycle of giving and receiving as only God can design.

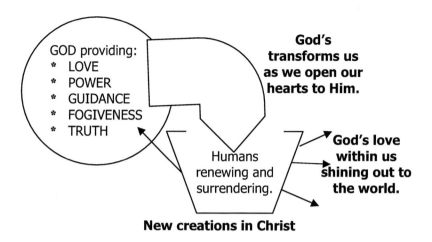

GOD providing:
* LOVE
* POWER
* GUIDANCE
* FOGIVENESS
* TRUTH

God's transforms us as we open our hearts to Him.

Humans renewing and surrendering.

God's love within us shining out to the world.

New creations in Christ

Once again He has set us up for success. God takes all the responsibility. He only asks that we relinquish the control of our fallen flesh to Him and He will use it for good.

I have a few little sayings I repeat to myself a lot. They help me keep my eyes on Christ. One of those little ditties I repeat to myself often is, "Lord, empty me of me and fill me with you." It helps me stay focused that my job is to simply get out of the way and allow Christ, who lives within me, to do His job. It's a beautiful thing when that happens.

PUTTING ON THE NEW MAN

Step four is about the process of putting on our "new man"; repeatedly surrendering the rest of our human core to God and letting Him complete the work He has already begun in us.

> *If indeed you have heard Him and have been taught by Him, as the truth is in Jesus: that you put off, concerning your former conduct, the old man which grows corrupt according to the deceitful lusts, and be renewed in the spirit of your mind, and that you put on the new man which was created according to God, in true righteousness and holiness.*
> *Ephesians 4:21-24 NKJV*

Our new man has a spirit of righteousness and holiness which comes directly from God.

There's a Monster Under My Bed

God does not change. We can count on His truths whether we believe them yet or not. The truth is the truth no matter what our minds, emotions or programmed perceptions tell us.

For example, children who are terrified of the dark completely believe that something bad will happen once the lights are turned off. No matter what you show, them they still believe the lie. "See honey, I'll turn the lights on. There isn't anything there." Still, they don't believe they are safe and the minute those lights go off, the fear overtakes them again. You can even leave a night light on. It does little to convince them. The truth is that they are safe, yet the fear becomes fully engrained into their heart, even though it has no basis in reality.

Even as adults we believe things that simply aren't true. But, we cling to them with such ferocity, they ARE truth to us. No matter what others tell us or show us, we still hold on to them. (I know something will happen even when the lights are on!) They are so deeply embedded in our binary code we act and react from them as if they were reality. (I will prolong going to bed. I will make up excuses so that I don't have to sleep in my own bed. I will throw a fit if the lights get turned off.) Our pre-programming has distorted our view of reality and causes us to behave in a way that may be ungodly.

Nope, Nope, I Don't Believe It!

Even when we are shown the truth, we can't seem to believe what we see with our own eyes. An anorexic person can't see themselves as thin. A man who was told as a child, "You will never amount to anything", can't believe he is successful even when he has achieved great wealth. It may never be enough for him to believe that he has amounted to something. The girl who was told, "You are ugly", grows into a lovely woman who can't stop going to the plastic surgeon because she can't be beautiful enough. Even some of the disciples could hardly believe their eyes when the newly resurrected Christ showed up for dinner. Thomas had to touch His scarred hands to believe.

For years, I've been plagued with a fear which has kept me distant in my relationships. Because of my fear of getting close to others, I trained myself to never have to rely on anyone else. I programmed myself to be totally self-sufficient. "I can do it myself. Thank you!"

I thought of God as someone to help me out only if I was too weak to handle the situation alone. I envisioned Him shaking His head and saying, "I have to bail you out again?!?" I had become very good at controlling my life, keeping myself safe, and doing all the right things so that I would never have to call upon God or anyone else. I believed if I colored within the lines, I would have peace. I thought it was about my own performance.

I remember the first time I recognized the lie. Through friends willing to be honest with me and a wonderful Bible study we were doing, God was there revealing just how much my behavior had damaged my relationships. He showed me the lie I had been clinging to – I didn't think I was worthy of being loved.

I don't exactly know where the lie came from or when I started to believe it. I can think back to times it caused me to drive people away from me. I thought that if I let anyone get too close to me they'd see how unworthy I was and reject me. I even ran from God. However, moment by moment, day by day, God has helped me replace the lie with the truth that I am worthy because He loves me. By His love, I am healed.

The Truth According to Yoda

"Putting on the new man" means we must reprogram ourselves to accept God's truth. We need to "unlearn" the lies planted within us (the old man) and relearn the truth, and so, change our programming. In the movie, *The Empire Strikes Back*, Yoda shows Luke what this means. The scene opens as Luke's tie-fighter begins to sink into the swamp....

> *Luke*: "We'll never get it out now."
> *Yoda*: "So certain are you. Always with you it cannot be done. Hear nothing that I say?"
> *Luke*: "Master, moving stones around is one thing. This is totally different."
> *Yoda*: Jabbing his walking stick into the ground. "No! No different! Only different in your mind. You must unlearn what you have learned."
> *Luke*: Stares at Yoda for a moment, trying to understand what he meant, then sighs. "Oh, all right, I'll give it a try." And turns toward the ship.
> *Yoda*: "NO! Try not – DO or do not. There is no try."
> Luke sighs and puts his hand out toward the ship and closes his eyes. The ship starts to move but then he loses concentration and it goes back down. He sits down defeated.
> *Luke*: "I can't, it's too big." As he gasps for breath.
> *Yoda*: Not giving in so easily. "Size matters not. Judge me by my size, do you?"

Luke shakes his head.

Yoda: "And where you should not. For my ally is the force. And a powerful ally it is. Life creates it – makes it grow. Its energy surrounds us and binds us. Luminous beings are we... not this crude matter (pinching Luke's flesh.) You must feel the force around you. Here between me and you – the tree – the rock - everywhere! Yes – even between the land and the ship."

Luke: "You want the impossible!" And gets up and walks to another place to sulk.

Yoda sighs and turns toward the ship. And quietly closes His eyes and uses the force to bring Luke's ship back to land.

Luke is awed and amazed. He has to touch the ship to make sure it is real.

Luke: "I don't believe it!"

Yoda: "THAT is why you fail."

Then Jesus said to the disciples, "Have faith in God. I can assure you that you can say to this mountain, "May God lift you up and throw you into the sea," and your command will be obeyed. All that is required is that you really believe and don't doubt in your heart. Mark 11:22-23 NLT

Exactly How Big is a Mustard Seed?

Nothing is too big for God to handle. Once someone told me, "You put God into a very small box." What they meant is that I put too many limitations on God's power. I used to think of His power as something confined by physical laws. God lives in the spiritual realm. He is not limited by anything we can see, touch, or taste. His only limit is our unwillingness to believe His truth. We must stop thinking so small, and start realizing God's immense capacity.

Do not fool yourself. If anyone thinks he knows a lot about the things of this world, he had better become a fool. Then he may become wise.
1 Corinthians 3:18 NLV

The only way to "put on the new man" is to let go of what we know of this world (the "old man"), unlearn what we think we know of humanity and input God's truths over and over again. What we used to think impossible, could be very possible with God (Mark 10:27). Jesus also told us that if we only had the faith the size of a mustard seed that we could do miraculous things (Matthew 17:20).

He wants us to continually input this truth into our human core until we think and act differently. Unlearn the lies, and relearn the truth; over and over, until we believe it. Repeat it until His truth is so fully enmeshed into our human core that we KNOW it to be true. Then we are no longer blinded to the truth. Our hearts need to be reprogrammed to view the world with "eternal eyes".

Could You Repeat That Please?

I used to think that all of this should have just magically happened somehow when I became a Christian. I felt guilty because I still had trouble surrendering. I tried and tried and still sank back into old patterns. I would feel centered and grounded only to fall apart when the situation became less predictable to me. When the situation or relationship would have even a small "bump along the road", it would represent that I hadn't done a good enough job at keeping everything safe. My programming told me to believe I had failed in some way.

I can tell that I'm wrestling with this when I'm feeling overwhelmed and unworthy. I continually renew my mind to the truth that God is worthy. He is in control. He is working in every situation and is not surprised by even the biggest pot holes in the road. The responsibility to lead me rests on His shoulders. My only responsibility is to follow. God is my source of strength. I've been repeating it until now, it has become a habit for me.

THE RHYTHM OF THE WALK

This is our Christian journey. Why else do you think God wants us to be in constant prayer? Why does He ask us to crack our Bible open and read the Living Word each day? Why does He create a schedule by giving us night and day? He set a cycle for the week that for six days we work and on the seventh day we rest. Each year we go through 12 moons and four seasons. Why else would He give us a rhythm to our lives; infancy, youth, coming of age, adulthood, middle age, golden years and death? God designed our lives with rhythm in repetition.

It may take an entire lifetime of repetition to find peace. We may struggle with one aspect of surrender for years. You may repeat these steps over thousands of times. But to God, it is only a split second of time. What we think of as an eternity with our human understanding, is really only a breath in God's Kingdom.

LORD, remind me how brief my time on earth will be. Remind me that my days are numbered, and that my life is fleeing away. My life is no

longer than the width of my hand. An entire lifetime is just a moment to
you: human existence is but a breath.   *Psalm 39:4-5 NLT*

Are We There Yet?

We may think of our life as a hectic, chaotic race to get from one goal to another. So often our lives become about the "can't wait's". We can't wait until we can learn to ride a bike. Soon we can't wait until school starts only to find ourselves counting the days until summer. We can't wait until we graduate and get a real job. After we get the job, we wonder when our next day off is going to be. We might think our lives will be complete once we find our mate.

Once the wedding is over, we think about that first house to call our own. The birth of our first child seems to take forever. Soon the years seem to start coming faster and life becomes more and more of a blur. Soon, we can't wait until the years slow down. We can get so lost in the "can't wait's" that we forget about the here and now moments. We lose so much of our lives looking toward tomorrow.

The "What If" Plague

Or, we spend too much time looking behind us regretting the days we've lost. "What if I things would have happened differently?" "What if I hadn't made so many mistakes?" "What if my dad (or mom) had treated me better?" "What if my spouse hadn't cheated on me?" Our eyes are glued to the rear-view mirror and we miss seeing the road we're on.

God implores us to look at the present, the day we have been gifted with. He wants us to realize He is working in this very moment; He's engaged in our lives with every breath we take. He is heavily involved with every aspect of our lives and is totally dependable.

Steep your life in God-reality, God-initiative, God-provisions. Don't
worry about missing out. You'll find all your everyday human concerns
will be met. Give your entire attention to what God is doing right now,
and don't get worked up about what may or may not happen tomorrow.
God will help you deal with whatever hard things come up when the time
comes.   *Matthew 6:33-34 The Message*

Is That It?

God intends for us to come to Him each day with our human frailties. He wants to continue to expose the lies to us so His truth can become deeply engrained within us. He wants us to focus on what He is doing right now in our lives and He asks us to sacrifice more of ourselves to His plan. When we do this, we acknowledge Him as the creator and giver of life. We show Him we trust Him completely with every aspect of our lives. Thus, our relationship deepens and God can accomplish more of His plan through us. That's it – the Christian walk. We will never find true and lasting peace in any other pursuit.

Life becomes much easier once we cast away all the distractions of the world and look at our very core – how God created us to be. Without these distractions, we can clearly see our purpose and His plan. Nothing is more important than following Christ's lead in our lives.

I once thought all these things were so very important, but now I consider them worthless because of what Christ has done. Yes, everything else is worthless when compared with the priceless gain of knowing Christ Jesus my Lord. I have discarded everything else, counting it all as garbage, so that I may have Christ and become one with Him. I no longer count on my own goodness or my ability to obey God's law, but I trust Christ to save me. For God's way of making us right with Himself depends on faith.   *Philippians 3: 7-9 NLT*

Not a Puppet on a String

Even when we have our attention centered on the day, Satan will try to blind us from God's truths with our problems. Satan will try to get us so overwhelmed and absorbed by our circumstances that we cannot focus on God. If our situation in life seems impossible, we can become hopeless. Once this happens, we become victims of those circumstances because we have become enslaved to them. We cry, "I can't take it – it's too much!" We give up any hope. We fail because of what we don't believe God can do.

God wants us to dwell on the reality of His truth. Would there be any circumstance which God will not break through? Could there be any situation God won't make better? Is there anything we could mess up that God wouldn't turn out for good? The answer is, "YES!"

"WHAT??!" You say to yourself. "Did I read that right?" Of course you did. He will not break through if we do not let Him. He will not force us, we must allow Him to work. Again, we aren't puppets for Him to control. We have free-will. We have a choice.

He does it not by pushing us around but by working within us, His Spirit deeply and gently within us.   *Ephesians 3:20b The Message*

When we don't surrender ourselves to Him, we will find we have ultimately surrendered to Satan. It's one or the other. We either choose to follow Him or crucify Him. God wants our willful obedience. Think about it. God wants to lead us by loving influence, not coercion. It is the most loving thing to do.

WHEN WE DON'T BELIEVE

We can easily recognize when we don't believe God's truths. There will be plenty of evidence within our human core. We will find fear, anger and resentment which build upon hurts that haven't had the healing touch of God. We'll find pride, deceit and sin stemming from our need to fend for ourselves to find fulfillment. Our hearts will beat with impatience, discontentment and complacency because we aren't fulfilled. We plainly see disbelief in the lives of the disciples. They were fearful cowards before they surrendered to God's truths.

They doubted what they had seen Jesus do even after He had miraculously fed 5,000 people. The next time they needed food, they whined about where it was going to come from (Matthew 15:32-39). They squabbled amongst themselves to see who would be the greatest in Christ's eyes. They were so concerned with gaining more; they didn't realize what they already had (Matthew 20:20-28).

Judas had such a small understanding of God he was willing to betray His Savior to the hands of those who would kill Him. Judas believed that Jesus was to be King in all the glory of human understanding; castle, flowing robes, crowns and earthly power. When it was evident that Jesus wasn't going to attain this kind of power on earth and overthrow the current government, Judas could not see past this defeat. Judas failed because he could not believe (Mark 14:10-11).

The disciples fled in terror the minute the going got tough. John was the only one to stand with Mary to watch Jesus being crucified. Everyone else hid. Jesus had told them that God had a plan for each of their lives. Even after everything Jesus had shown them about His power and His Father's work, they were consumed with fear for what would happen to them at the hands of other humans (Matthew 26:56).

I'm Not Worried

Have you been there? Have you had such little faith in God that you let fear, doubt and unbelief overcome you? Have you been so caught up in your circumstances that you felt hopeless? We have all been there more times that we'd like to count. God says He is more than that. He is our great refuge. Believe with your heart and He will be our strength.

Do not worry. Learn to pray about everything. Give thanks to God as you ask Him for what you need. The peace of God is much greater than the human mind can understand. This peace will keep your hearts and minds through Christ Jesus.   *Philippians 4:6-7 NLV*

First of all, God knows you will have things you want to worry about. He says instead of worrying, take it to Him in prayer. While you are in prayer tell Him what you need and give thanks. Then, you will know peace; not "a peace", or "human peace", or "some peace". You will know "God's peace", which is more incredible than anyone can describe. It's our little slice of heaven God shows us here on earth.

God will be our refuge; He will guard and protect our hearts. It will be by His strength that we are safe as long as we are living in Christ Jesus. What does it mean to live in Christ Jesus? It means to continually surrender to Him as the leader of your life. Repeatedly unlearning the lies and relearning the truth about who He is and engraining it into our human core. It means living out our faith in Him in all we do.

WHEN WE BELIEVE

The disciples showed us a very different picture once they started living in Christ Jesus. Their peace surpassed anyone's understanding despite their seemingly hopeless circumstances. People from everywhere were seeking to annihilate them and constantly undermine their reputations. But, their faith and boldness remained unshakeable because of the truth that was planted within them.

Peter no longer ran away and denied his faith. He embraced it and lives were transformed from the strength that was pouring out from within him. He became so bold and unwavering and people responded to him in a mighty way. Thousands came to Christ through God working in Peter (The Book of Acts).

John began to grasp what Jesus had been trying to teach them about when He was living with them. Once John began to plant God's truths into his life, God began to open John's eyes to more of His mysteries. The book of John is filled with rich understandings of who Jesus was and what God was doing through Jesus. Some of the deepest prophetic truths of the Bible were revealed to John in the book of Revelation.

Paul had never met Jesus in the flesh, but, because of Paul's potential for faith, God invested much into his life. Paul (Saul) was off to crusade against Christians when his life completely changed. Knocked off his horse and blinded, Paul was left helpless and Jesus came to his rescue. Once Paul surrendered his heart, Christ took him on a three-year journey of unlearning the lies Paul believed and downloading the new truth into him. After that, everything about Paul reflected the truths that had engrained into his heart. He was a powerful tool to show others God's strength to change lives (Galatians 1:15-24).

It's So Bright I Have to Wear Shades!

Some of what life throws our way we truly can't help. However, I tend to believe the majority of the problems we encounter are related to our free-will choices not to follow Him. Don't despair though, God has promised that His love is sufficient to not only help us cope, but to give us victory over the situation. Even when we are dealing with the penalty of not "dropping our nets", He doesn't hold it against us or make us suffer alone.

Let's go back and rephrase some earlier questions. Is there any circumstance that God cannot break through? Is there any situation God can't make better? Could there be anything we mess up that God couldn't turn out for good? The answer is, "NO, when we are surrendered to Him."

The steps of the godly are directed by the LORD. He delights in every detail of their lives. Though they stumble, they will not fall, for the LORD holds them by the hand.　　　　　　　　*Psalm 37:23-24 NLT*

That is how God can promise that we are no longer slaves to our circumstances. We don't have to fear what life throws our way. We don't have to worry about yesterday's carry-overs, today's problems or tomorrow's fears. God is more powerful than anything in the universe. He even defeated death! And He has us covered by His eternal plan. All we have to do is allow Him to work it out in our lives. We need to give up the control. When we are weakest, God is our strength and power.

Through surrender we finally find what we've been lacking. We are no longer driven to fill our emptiness. We are finally freed from the chains of guilt and shame. We are no longer victims of our circumstances. We become content with what God is doing within our lives in the here and now. We are free! The way we act and react to those around us naturally becomes more loving, kind, and patient because of the peace and strength we are finding within our heart. The situations that used to render us helpless now become only an opportunity for God to show His power at work within us.

When Christ, who is our life, is revealed, then you also will be revealed with Him in glory.   *Colossians 3:4 NASB*

DOWNLOAD THE TRUTH

You may think I'm talking about brainwashing yourself into believing God's truths. It may sound like a technique used in cults to make their followers more submissive. In some ways, I *AM* talking about brainwashing. Believe it or not, you are being brainwashed every day, almost incessantly. Our brains are downloading lies from the Internet, TV, radio, newspaper, magazines, billboards, in stores, in the workplace and in restaurants. We can get influenced by almost every commercial we see.

Our kids are being brainwashed in schools, by computer games, by peers and other parents. Our beliefs are continually being influenced by the world around us. Can you guess the percentage of what you see, hear, experience is godly? How much of the "stuff" going into our human core relates God's truths?

If you aren't very careful of what you're downloading into your heart, you may find yourself subtly brainwashed into believing lies. Satan is extremely active in the world. He is the King of this world. If we aren't listening to God, we are listening to Satan.

Truth Exercise

Try this exercise for 30 days. The following is a list of truths. First, you'll need to copy them on an index card or input them into your organizer so you can carry them with you. Then repeat them out loud, at least once a day, for 30 consecutive days. Feel free to edit this list with truths that are meaningful to you.

- I am a precious child of God.
- I am perfectly loved by Christ.
- Christ is the master of my life. I relinquish all control to Him.
- He will never leave or forsake me.
- I don't need to fear anything because Christ is for me.
- He will work everything out for good as I surrender to Him.
- There is nothing too hard for God to handle.
- My life is about serving Him.
- He wants to be revealed through me and my circumstances.

- My goal is to consistently grow closer to Christ.
- Since Christ lives within me, I am whole and complete.
- I lack nothing. God provides all I need.
- God is limitless and He is with me right here, right now.
- I am worthy of love because of who He is.
- He is pure love and His Spirit fills me.
- Through His strength, I can love others unconditionally.
- Some day, I will be with Him in heaven for the rest of eternity.

After 30 days, check your level of peace. It should grow the more you ingrain these truths into your heart. Gradually, you begin to act and react based on their foundation.

We must make a commitment to repeat God's truths to ourselves every chance we get. Make a tape or CD to play in your car, write a journal about God's truths in your life to read each morning, pray out loud with your family before meals, discuss with your spouse. Consistently download God into your core. Refuse to let the culture of this world brainwash you into acting and reacting based on their lies. Focus on God and what He is doing in your life. Repeat these truths over and over, and surrender any resistance to God's plan for your life. It will bring you the peace that surpasses all understanding.

Fix these words of mine in your hearts and minds; tie them as symbols on your hands and bind them on your foreheads. Teach them to your children, talking about them when you sit at home and when you walk along the road, when you lie down and when you get up.

Deuteronomy 11:18-19 NIV

Questions to Ponder:

1. Why do we need to repeat the steps of surrender?

2. Why is it important to carefully guard what you watch, listen to, and experience?

3. What do you need to unlearn about God? What do you need to learn?

4. What steps are you going to commit to taking to renewing your mind?

CHAPTER EIGHT

THE ART
OF IT

The most untutored person with passion is more persuasive than the most eloquent without. François, Duc de La Rochefoucauld

I was awake the minute his foot hit the bottom step. My eyes were already open when he gently shook me and said, "It's time." He didn't have to tell me twice! I was out of the bed before his hand was off my shoulder.

I could hear the crickets still singing so I knew it was very early. My brothers moaned a little and turned over, murmuring something about "back to sleep", which meant that the morning was going to belong to just my dad and me.

I threw on the clothes that I had laid out the night before. I scoffed a little when I had to put on the sweatshirt my mom insisted on. Secretly, I was glad she made me wear one, because the mornings were always cooler than I expected. Once I was dressed, I snuck down the steps as quietly as the old cabin would allow.

Dad was there waiting for me with the fishing gear already lying beside the door. I knew the drill so Dad didn't have to say much. He took the lead and grabbed most of the stuff. I gathered the rest of the gear up and quietly closed the door behind me. Then I followed him as he headed toward the longest dock.

Just before we got to the dock, I took a quick look back at the cabin we rented almost every summer; just to make sure no one was going to join us. I was glad when Dad and I got the dock to ourselves.

We strategically placed the chairs in the configuration that would give us the best vantage point, with the safest, "Watch out, I'm going to cast" distance. Dad got my pole ready first. He knew that I was antsy to make my first cast. He understood that nine-year-olds weren't long on patience.

He whispered, "Hand me your pole." It was the only time we spoke. He carefully put the hook, sinker and bobbers on at the perfect spacing to keep my hook just below the water. That way I might be able to catch a glimpse of the fish as it took the bait.

One of my favorite things to do on our fishing trip was to reach in to the Styrofoam cup that was mostly filled with dirt and find a worm. I loved playing in the dirt and fishing out the worms. I didn't even mind putting the worm on the hook. It seemed very natural to me. Fish eat worms, so you put a worm on the hook. Once I had found my worm and secured it tightly to the hook, I was ready to cast.

Casting is a real art form. It takes lots of practice and loads of patience. I loved to hear the sound that the reel made when the line was going out. In fact, I would cast my line out and hope that it didn't cast well, so that I could reel it back in a try it again.

I was fascinated with the rhythm I could make; push the button, throw the rod back, flick it forward, let go of the button at just the right moment so that the line flew out freely. "WHIZZZZZ." Then you'd hear a "PLOP" when the line hit the water. Next, I would move the reel handle a little until you heard a "CLICK" which meant the line was locked. At that point, I was supposed to just sit and wait for the fish to bite. However, when you're nine, you tend to reel the line back in quickly so that you hear a "SQWEEEEE" sound and get to do it all over again. Push, throw, flick, let go, WHIZZZZZ, PLOP, CLICK, SQWEEEEEEEEE. It was my own little symphony of sounds.

I'm pretty sure that I spent more time casting and reeling in then I did fishing, but somehow it didn't matter. Dad tried to get me to leave my line in longer, but soon gave up and let me go back to my rhythm.

Once in awhile, I would just let the line sit. That was when I noticed the other sounds around me. I heard the water lap gently against the dock supports. And every so often, I heard the splash of a fish jumping. It was in one of those moments, in the stillness of the morning, that I felt peace for the first time. Sometimes you don't realize how loud life is until you experience something so calm. Even as a child I recognized this.

After awhile, I realized that the crickets had stopped chirping and now it was the birds turn to sing. Soon the sun started to come up and the birds sang louder. The sky was filled with such amazing colors that my breath caught in my chest as I watched them change. Sometimes, the water would glow as the sun would hit it and, if you squinted just right, I would swear that the water was turning soda-pop orange. Sometimes I had reach down and cup some in my hand, just to make sure it really wasn't fizzy pop.

All too soon, the sun would float farther up on the horizon and it would get too warm for the fish to be biting. Then the sounds of others waking up and getting going would start to drift through the air. Dad and I would start talking louder and moving a little faster. The stillness was gone. Pretty soon, we packed up and headed back to the cabin for breakfast.

I remember many times dropping my gear off at the door and looking back toward the water. My heart would once again fill with that incredible feeling of peace. I felt powerful, yet completely calm. It was like I knew something that the others didn't. It was gift that I got to take with me for the rest of the day.

It was an incredible feeling. I felt a warmth in my stomach that would rise up and gradually overtake my whole body. As a small child, those fishing trips were when I thought the most about God. I knew there was a God and that I was feeling very close to Him sitting out there on the dock. Part of the peace I felt came from the stillness of the morning and part of it came from being with my father. I felt safe and secure to be out in the wilderness because he was by my side, taking care of me just as my Heavenly Father does. I lost track of that when I was a teenager. But, now as an adult, I think back to those times with great fondness.

GOD'S PEACE

My early morning fishing trips gave me a glimpse of what I have found in Christ. He offers us something even more incredible. When we passionately surrender our lives to Him, He passionately supplies us with peace. Not just any peace – God's peace; tranquility, serenity, stillness, quiet assurance, complete satisfaction within our hearts. He *IS* the God of peace. When we experience His peace, we are forever changed. Once we have been given this gift, we can't help but want others to experience it as well. It's that powerful.

> *"The LORD bless you*
> *and keep you;*
> *the LORD make his face shine upon you*
> *and be gracious to you;*
> *the LORD turn his face toward you*
> *and give you peace."*　　　　　　　*Numbers 6:24-26 NIV*

When Jesus asked a couple of lowly fishermen to follow Him, He didn't even have to tell them what they would get out of the deal. They just sensed something incredible would happen if they dropped their nets, left the life they knew, and followed this man wherever He went. To become "fishers of men" must have intrigued them enough to push doubts aside and press forward. They were richly rewarded for their faith. Many incredible things did indeed happen along their journey.

The goal of our journey is not to be happy or comfortable. It's about learning to totally surrender all we have, all we are and all we aren't to Christ. God will teach us how to do this when we are happy and comfortable. He can also teach us by allowing circumstances in our lives which make us unhappy and uncomfortable. We'll learn when we are experiencing great success, great failures, deep fears or sorrows. God can use all of what life offers to teach us the lesson of surrender.

No, this journey is definitely not about being comfortable. It's about passion and peace. It's about single-mindedly giving ourselves to Christ so that we can partake in His peace. It's about clinging desperately to something, then having enough faith to let go and allow Christ to break its hold over you. It's about freedom.

Keep putting into practice all you learned from me and heard from me and saw me doing, and the God of peace will be with you.
Philippians 4:9 NIV

THE ART OF CASTING

Before Peter and Andrew became followers of Christ, they were fishermen. The best time to fish was at night. So, they would gather at the shore in the evening and ready their boats and nets. Then they would row out in their boats and drop their nets into the Sea of Galilee.

There was an art to dropping the nets. If they did it too quickly or too slowly the fish would be swim away. They would have to drop them in a large curve with the open side facing the shore in order to get the best haul of fish. Their ability or inability to cast their nets determined how many fish they caught.

It took practice. They would start as young children going out occasionally with their fathers and brothers to learn the trade. At first, they wouldn't catch a thing. They would expend a lot of energy and accomplish very little. But, gradually they learned just the right way to flip their wrists and toss their shoulders to get the best curve in the net. And soon, they would be hauling in a sizeable catch.

Even experienced fishermen, for whatever reason, would cast their nets out awkwardly from time to time. Call it a mental slip or a momentary lack of good judgment. But, they would haul them back in and try again.

This is how it is with surrender. There is an art to it. It takes practice and perseverance. We may not be able to do it very well at first. It may feel very awkward and difficult to do. But, over time, we learn how to do it better. And sometimes, even when you've been surrendering to God's lead on a daily basis, you get a little side-tracked and lose your perspective. All God asks us to do is to try again.

> *Patient endurance is what you need now, so you will continue to do God's will. Then you will receive all that he has promised.*
> *Hebrews 10:36 NLT*

Christ-Like Pottery

> *"In your hands, the pain and hurt feel less like scars*
> *And more like character." Sara Groves*

We must realize that God is building our character, molding and shaping us into who He intended us to be. It doesn't necessarily feel good to be molded. However, in the hands of the potter, we become beautiful pieces of pottery.

> *As the clay is in the potters hand, so you are in my hand.*
> *Jeremiah 18:6b NLT*

That is His purpose for our day-to-day struggles and successes. He is using them to gradually mold us into who He created us to be. He created us to be mirrors of Christ. He wants people to see His reflection when they look at us. It takes time and patience on both sides. God patiently working in our lives and us patiently persevering in the journey.

What's awesome and quite astounding is that He uses us throughout our journey. He can use us where we are today, with all the out of shape clay in our lives – *if* we let Him. Many of us think He won't be able to use us until we are perfect. He wants to use *imperfect* vessels. It's not about our performance; rather life is about *His* performance through our flaws. Our weakness is always perfected in His grace and strength when we are surrendered. That's when people see Christ in us – when He is at work in our lives. He has given us help from every angle so that the only way we can fail is by not surrendering.

That is why, for Christ's sake, I delight in weaknesses, in insults, in hardships, in persecutions, in difficulties. For when I am weak, then I am strong.　　　　　　　　　　　　　　　　　　*2 Corinthians 12:10 NIV*

GETTING IN THE BOAT

The only way for God to mold us the way He wants is for us to surrender everything we are to Him. The whole thing, all of us, placed in His hands to shape as He sees fit. He knows we aren't perfect but He still wants to use us.

The best way to learn anything is by doing it. You can't drive a car by reading a manual. You must get behind the wheel, turn it on, put it into gear and step on the gas. You can't catch any fish until you get into the boat and cast your nets.

Satan tries to keep us from doing just that. He tells us over and over again that we will never be good or worthy enough. He tricks us into thinking we must hide our imperfections. We must be ashamed of our weaknesses. Satan never wants us to behind the wheel. He knows that God will meet us there and help us. Satan doesn't want us to know that. Satan loves to use our ignorance, fear and shame to keep us hiding in the darkness. But, God asks us to get out there and cast.

Don't hide you light under a basket! Instead, put it on a stand and let it shine for all.　　　　　　　　　　　　　　　　*Matthew 5:15 NLT*

I don't necessarily feel like I shine very often. Some parts of me are fairly bright, I guess, but most parts aren't much to look at. The more I give of myself to God, the more Christ is revealed from within me and *those* pieces are really shiny. All I have to do is stop blocking the light.

I think I'm Getting the Hang of It

We may not be very good at first. It might take a lot of practice until we get the hang of it. We just need to keep working. Never getting behind the wheel again after you have an accident doesn't make you a better driver. Trying it again while being more alert and aware does improve your skills. Before long, it becomes part of who we are. We don't even have to consciously think about it anymore. It's just natural. It begins feeling less like scars and more like character. That's what Paul was experiencing when he wrote:

I can do all things through Christ who strengthens me.
Philippians 4:13 NKJV

Paul practiced surrendering his hunger, exhaustion, fear and his success to God until it was just a natural response for him. He knew that no matter what life threw him, he would be able to surrender it and God would come through for Him. Paul had repeated this truth until he knew it in his very core. He didn't let Satan's lies or his own insecurities interfere with God's work. He fought the battle, ran the race, and learned through it all who God is. The more Paul gave of himself, the more God was able to reveal Christ through him. All the extra clay was molded away until an incredibly beautiful piece of art was revealed. However, Paul didn't get there by sitting at the sea shore. He was in the boat relentlessly casting his nets!

THE TACKLE BOX

God has already given us all of the tools we need to be an expert fisherman. Everything that we could ever need to have a flourishing relationship with Christ is at our fingertips. We just need to look into God's tackle box.

The Holy Spirit is the sonar. The Holy Spirit is on constant vigil, keeping watch for jagged rocks which could damage our boat or for the school of fish waiting for us to catch. It's our guide and truth monitor.

The Bible is our step-by-step, how-to guide for any kind of fishing situation. Whether calm or stormy sea, plenty or few fish, catfish or Blue Marlin, our answers are written in His Word.

Our worship of God can be as varied as a wide assortment of lures. Lures can be fancy, down-to-earth, used for slow motion or promote a flurry of activity.

A fishing technique that gets handed down from generation to generation is the art of visualization. This is where you clearly visualize the perfect cast in your mind's eye before you actually cast. We can also use imagery to help us see our relationships flourish in our mind before living them out.

Holy Spirit

Our sonar helps safely guide us to the most bountiful fishing grounds. It is our most powerful tool. The Holy Spirit comes to dwell within our spirit the moment we allow Christ to be the leader of our lives. The Holy Spirit never leaves us. It provides the truth through revelation to us. The Holy Spirit is our link to the living God.

But when the Father sends the Counselor as my representative – and by the Counselor I mean the Holy Spirit – He will teach you everything and remind you of everything I myself have told you. John 14:26 NLT

He counsels, comforts, prays for us with groanings which only God can understand. The empty place we try so hard to fill with worldly things is totally and completely consumed by His Spirit. Its power is available to us at all times from within us. The more we draw from its power, the more Christ is revealed to the world.

The Bible

God gave us the Bible to provide us with instructions for our daily lives. It is written by God using men as His ink pen. We can access God's truth, get encouragement, gain wisdom and be convicted through the scriptures. The Word is wisdom. It keeps us on the right path. It is alive; living and breathing. It cuts to our very core in ways that nothing else can. When we experience the scriptures, we taste God. It is the only book we will ever read that gives us more each time we open it.

God's Word is living and powerful. It is sharper than a sword that cuts both ways. It cuts straight into where the soul and spirit meet and it divides them. It cuts into the joints and bones. It tells what the heart is thinking about and what it wants to do. Hebrews 4:12 NLV

Great comfort and strength can be found by studying and memorizing His Word. Praying the scriptures is another valuable tool. You pray a scripture silently or out loud and replace the pronouns with the name of who you are praying for. For example, take Philippians 2:13 and replace the pronoun, "you" with "me", therefore making it personal. "For God is working in me, giving me the desire to obey Him and the power to do what pleases Him." Repeating this prayer is a powerful way to renew your mind to this truth.

Worship

Worship is what "lures" us to Christ. We can worship through things like music, dance and fellowship. The angels sing God's praises without stopping. David sang and danced to show His love for God. Music can reach our very core. God delights in it! He wants us to enjoy the gift of music with our fingers – playing instruments, with our voices – singing loudly to the Lord, and with our bodies – dancing and rejoicing in all He has given us.

> *Let them praise His name with dancing and make music to Him with tambourine and harp.*   *Psalm 149:3 NIV*

There are influential churches of all sizes out there that are alive and powerfully representing the body of Christ. The fellowship found there is inspiring! They can greatly help you in worship. Do you belong to one?

There are also very dead churches out there that seem to suck the life out of you. Do you belong to one of those? God wants us to be excited to go to church, fellowship with other believers, and participate in worship. He wants us to view worship as more than just an obligation we fulfill on Sundays. The early church was alive with worship. The brothers and sisters in Christ worked hard to support and encourage each other.

> *God knows how much I love you and long for you with the tender compassion of Christ Jesus.*   *Philippians 1:8 NLT*

We can offer everything that we do as an offering to God. We can worship Him with our work, with the way we love our family and friends, with the way we keep our houses clean, with the way we take care of our bodies. As long as we are surrendered to Christ, our lives can be given in an act of worship.

Imagery

> *In my mind's eye, I can see your face*
> *As your love pours down in a shower of grace... DC Talk*

God knows that our minds can vividly imagine something godly or embrace something sinful. Once the picture is firmly entrenched in our minds, the next step is to act it out. If you vividly imagine a deep relationship with Christ, then you are much closer to achieving the "perfect cast."

> *For those who are according to the flesh set their minds on the things of the flesh, but those who are according to the Spirit, the things of the Spirit.*   *Romans 8:5 NASB*

We can absorb pictures better than words. Jesus knew this and painted many pictures through His parables to capture our imagination. Most of what He taught was in the form of imagery. Many times, the best sermons are the ones where the pastor paints a clear picture we can relate to. We see it with our hearts. The more vivid the picture, the more our brains can remember it. A picture which lies to us, (as the anorexic stares into the mirror and sees a fat person) can seem so real because we have imagined it to be real. We must replace the distorted pictures with true ones. For example, what would happen in your heart if you reflected on this image often?

I saw my Father with his arms stretched out waiting for me to come close. With a slight hesitation I stepped toward Him. When I was within His reach, His hands gently touched my chin and He lifted my head to gaze into my eyes. With such a gentle and compassionate touch, I felt it was safe to look back and when my eyes met with His, calmness came over me. Tenderly, His hands moved down and came to rest on my shoulders. With sweetness and yet authority, He spoke these words to me: "Believe what I tell you my dear child. Be strong and courageous, do the work I have called you to do. Don't be afraid or discouraged by the size of the task, for I am with you always. I will never fail you and I will never forsake you."

My eyes swelled with tears as I gazed into His eyes and listened to His words. Then in silence He drew me unto Himself and I stepped even closer, welcoming His warm embrace. As His loving arms surrounded me I could do nothing more than rest my head upon His chest. Yes, this is what I long for. This is where I want to stay. This is God's desire for me; that I rest in the security of His embrace and allow His love to fill me and flow through me. [4]

There's an image that I try to remain focused on when I'm with other people. I think of myself as wearing a full-body suit. The suit looks just like me from the outside. Same color hair, skin and eyes. Same imperfections, but they have no hold on me anymore because I know what really lies beneath the suit. I take the truth with me wherever I go. When I want to unveil the truth, I simply unzip the suit and let it drop away. What is revealed underneath is breathtaking to all who behold it. A brilliant light is shining from within me. Everyone has to shield their eyes even though they can't help but keep staring at its brightness. There is something in that light that they have been longing for. Something within its rays that calls to them, stirs their hearts and makes them feel something they have been starved for – love. Perfect, complete, consuming love like they have never known. I have simply shown them what is inside of me – Christ in all of His beauty. I stripped away everything people thought I was to reveal the truth of who I am in Christ.

Replace negative pictures in your mind's eye with the beautiful images that Christ has waiting for you. Unlearn the old, and relearn the new. Reprogram your binary code to accept God's reality. Ask Him to help open your eyes to see the new image in your mirror.

Our human core will transform as we actively marinate ourselves in God's truth. Our God-given tackle box is the best available to mankind. It's at right at our fingertips. Have you opened the lid lately?

THE TUG-OF-WAR

You might feel torn. This sounds like truth to you. You want to believe it, but something keeps nagging at you; some fear, or resentment, or temptation that is pulling you back and holding you hostage. You might be carrying on a knock-down drag-out fight deep inside. It's almost like you have the little white angel on one shoulder and the little red devil on the other battling it out.

All of these thoughts and feelings are perfectly natural and human. In fact, we won't escape them. We can't change the fact that we are human. We can only learn to surrender our humanness to God and allow Him to do the rest. Go to step one and start from the beginning. God will be there and peace will come.

No Light at the End of the Tunnel

You might be saying, "But you don't understand! My situation is hopeless. How can I not be afraid about what is going to happen?"

I'm sure I don't understand. But, I know that God does. He knows you; He knows what's happened, what is happening now, and what will happen. He has a plan worked out to carry you through despite your circumstances. Trust Him, believe Him and follow Him. Dive into His word. Pray to Him. Acknowledge His power and love for you each day.

Prayer for you: "Lord, I'm fearful, but I know that you are completely in control. I will surrender to Your Plan. Lead me through this storm, because I am sinking in the waves. I know

101

You love me and You will provide a way out because I believe in Your truth. I pray you work through these circumstances in a miraculous way – but I know that You will rescue me in Your way and Your timing. I praise you Lord!"

Some verses for you to claim: Psalm 27, Psalm 112, Proverbs 3

Hurt, Broken and Lost

You might be saying, "You have no idea how much I've been hurt in my life. So many people have lied to me, abused and neglected me. How can I forgive them?!! When is God going to take revenge for my pain??"

Humans inflict so much pain and suffering on each other. Lies, abuse and neglect are horrific things to experience. The left-over scars make forgiveness very hard. Forgiving means releasing the ones who hurt you from the consequences of the abuse. It means letting go of your bitterness and the other person's sins against you – whether the other person deserves it or not. Forgiveness does not mean to forget. It only means to not hold the other person accountable for their sin toward you. In doing so however, you get released from their sin's hold on you too. Then God can restore and heal you.

Prayer for you: "Lord, I've been so deeply wounded. I've felt this pain and bitterness in my very core for so long, I don't know what it will feel like to be released from them. I'm not even sure I will know how to live without them. Holding onto my anger makes me feel safe, somehow. I know these are lies. I know Your healing is greater than anything I've ever felt. I'm not sure I even feel worthy of the release. But, I do know that You are the great counselor and comforter. And I know that You are the King of the broken hearted. I trust you with my wounds. I forgive those who have hurt me. I release my pain to You. I praise You for Your loving ways!"

Some verses for you to claim: Acts 3:16, Matthew 6:12-15, Matthew 18:20-22, Colossians 3:13

I Wouldn't Change a Thing

"Life is really good right now. I'm really comfortable. Things are going well. I have no fears or doubts, I feel really safe. Surely God would want things to stay even keel like this? Why would I want to rock the boat?"

Praise God that you are experiencing so many blessings! Rejoice in your comfort! Live in the moment you have been given and sing of God's mighty provision in your life. Each day ask God how He wants to use your blessing in His work. Willingly give of anything God has graciously given to you if He asks! Be sure to give the praise and honor to the One who has been leading.

> Prayer for you: "Lord, thank You so much for being so kind and merciful toward me. I praise You for all that you are doing in my life. Help me keep my focus on You so I do not get too comfortable or too safe. I want to do Your will. I do not want to get caught up in my comfort so that I resist when You lead me elsewhere that may not be as comfortable. I will not fear that because I know You will be with me always. I will trust in You and Your plan for my life. Thank you Lord for being my strength! Some verses for you to claim: Job 22:21, Proverbs 1:32, Psalm 105:1, Psalm 139:23

I Still Don't Get It

"I'm still confused. How can I tell if God is leading me or Satan is? How can I know God's will for my life? I've messed up before when I thought I was surrendering. I keep trying but can't seem to figure it out."

All of us have "messed up". We all have been led astray. Don't worry! You don't have to be perfect for God to use you. God knows our hearts. All He wants is a sincere heart and persistence! Most of the stories in the Bible relate to humans who've gone astray at some point in their walk with God. God can even use our slip-ups to further His glory. He will continue His work in you if you just keep at it.

> Prayer for you: "My Father, I'm unsure and hesitant. I don't want to mess up. I want to surrender to Your will, but I'm not sure how to do it. Please be very obvious with me so I can tell the difference between You, Satan or me. I get confused. Show me what I am missing. I know that You will lead me. I sincerely ask You to guide and direct me to Your path. You'll need to mark it with neon lights so I can see it clearly. Help build my confidence and reliance upon You. If there is something that I am doing that You want me to stop, You have my permission to show it to me. If there is something I should be doing that I am not, I allow You to bring it to my attention in any way You need to for me to take notice. I'm going to take each day as it comes and do the best I know how. And when I do mess up, I allow You to turn it out for

good. Train my eyes to see Your handiwork! I praise You for Your trustworthiness and for being so active in my life!" Some verses for you to claim: Exodus 4:12-15, Job 34:32, Psalm 32:7-9, Psalm 86:11, Luke 12:12

THE ART OF PERSERVERENCE

If you are struggling to love God with all of heart, don't give up, don't lose heart, and don't give in to despair or complacency. True and lasting peace comes from the journey. We take a baby step, and God helps move us a mile. Each time we see God's mighty hand at work, we find more strength to keep moving forward. The more we give of ourselves, the more Christ can work through us. Passionately seek the truth that comes from Jesus Christ and press on.

We are hard pressed on every side, but not crushed; perplexed, but not in despair; persecuted, but not abandoned; struck down, but not destroyed.
                                                          2 Corinthians 4:8-9 NIV

This life can be very hard. We can feel defeated. We may face many battles. The more we follow Christ, the more fiery arrows Satan will sling at us (Ephesians 6:10-20). God will allow us to suffer as He sees fit for our growth. We don't grow nearly as well in successes as we do in struggles. But, He will always be there to help us along, carry us through and provide miracles just when we need them.

We must realize that, just as with the rest of our lives, there is a rhythm to our journey – it will ebb and flow. (Sometimes we will be fed, sometimes not fed, loved or unloved, healthy or ill. Sometimes we will have plenty and other times we won't have enough.) All the while, we can be assured that God gives us just what we need.

The goal is not comfort or happiness. The goal is to grow closer to Christ so that God's plan can be fulfilled through us. The art of it is to never give up. If we fail, God will cover us if we let Him. He will turn all things out for good for those who are called according to His purpose for them (Romans 8:28). He has begun a work in us and He will persevere until it's completed. The only thing He asks is to not resist. When we surrender to Him He gives us peace, joy, love and innumerable blessings in returns.

The more we give of ourselves, the more He gives Himself to us, the more we can experience His peace. And there is great power in that. We truly become strong when we are weak. When we empty ourselves of our human frailties, He can fill us with His strength. His plan was designed for

His glory and for our benefit. His plan for you is totally unique. It has a completely different rhythm than anyone else's. Watching God as He sculpts you into a breathtaking piece of art is a wondrous process to behold. The others around you are drawn to the sweetness of its beauty. It captivates them and gradually draws them into the potter's hand as He begins the process in their lives. It's His good and perfect will for our lives here on earth. Breathe it in and embrace it. Live it out from your human core and rejoice in it!

WHAT'S YOUR PASSION?

So, you've seen the Garden of Eden and know what it's like to feel naked and alone. You've seen the Garden of Gethsemane and see how to "get real", surrender yourself to God and receive powerful peace which is beyond our imagination. You've briefly seen God from behind as He passed before your gaze. We know He has more loving thoughts for us than there are grains of sand. We understand all God wants from us – "drop our nets" and follow Him.

I pray that you drop whatever you are clinging to and grab a hold of God with all the passion you have within your heart. I pray that you will continually renew your mind to the truth God has planted deep within you. I pray that you live in His peace that surpasses all understanding. Allow Him to use you as He transforms the lives of those you touch. All of this is only a surrender away.

I have heard of your faith in the Lord Jesus and your love for all Christians. Since then, I always give thanks for you and pray for you. I pray that the great God and Father of our Lord Jesus Christ may give you the wisdom of His Spirit. Then you will be able to understand the secrets about Him as you know Him better.

I pray that your hearts will be able to understand. I pray that you will know about the hope given by God's call. I pray that you will see how great the things are that He has promised to those who belong to Him.

I pray that you will know how great His power is for those who have put their trust in Him. It is the same power that raised Christ from the dead. This same power put Christ at God's right side in heaven.

This place was given to Christ. It is much greater than any king or leader can have. No one else can have this place of honor and power. No

one in this world or in the world to come can have such honor and
power.   *Ephesians 1:15-21 NLV*

Questions to Ponder:

1. What are some tools in "God's Tackle Box" to help us in our journey? Why are they important?

2. Which of these tools do you use well? Which one(s) do you want to use more often?

3. In what ways is surrender an art?

4. Define and then write at least three commitments you are willing to make today that will help you passionately surrender your life to Christ:

NOTES

DROP YOUR NETS AND FOLLOW ME
1. John Marquez, *The Christ-Life Solution, "It is Finished!"* (Des Moines: Christ-Life Ministries, Inc., 2001), p.136.
2. Robert Kessler et al, "The Epidemiology of Major Depressive Disorder: Results From the National Comorbidity," *JAMA*, (2003), 289:3095-3105.

KNOW GOD
3. C.S. Lewis, *Mere Christianity* (New York: Macmillian Publishing Co., 1952), 1967.

THE ART OF IT
4. Imagery written by my dear friend, Shirley Sterk.